The Islamists Are Coming

The Islamists Are Coming

Who They Really Are

Robin Wright, Editor

Woodrow Wilson Center Press
United States Institute of Peace Press
Washington, DC

EDITORIAL OFFICES

Woodrow Wilson Center Press
Woodrow Wilson International Center for Scholars
One Woodrow Wilson Plaza
1300 Pennsylvania Avenue, N.W.
Washington, DC 20004-3027
Telephone: 202-691-4029
www.wilsoncenter.org

ORDER FROM

United States Institute of Peace Press
PO Box 605
Herndon, VA 20172
Telephone: 800-868-8064; 703-661-1590
Fax: 703-661-1501
www.usip.org

Library of Congress Cataloging-in-Publication Data Applied For
ISBN paperback   978-1-60127-134-1
ISBN ePub   978-1-60127-135-8

Contents

Foreword

This timely book showcases what the Wilson Center and United States Institute of Peace do best: the blending of practical scholarship and policy to tackle urgent, complex issues in a "safe political space." Surely the rise of Islam as a political force is one such issue.

Scarcely more than a year ago, virtually no one predicted the speed and breadth of a grassroots surge that has toppled governments across the Middle East and required those still standing to make hasty changes to accommodate the fierce winds of change. At the time of writing, Syria remains the only Arab country to scorn worldwide pressure. Most governments, the European Union, and the Arab League have condemned its leader, and few expect him and his government to survive. Indeed, the demands for dignity and fairness are heard in the streets of Moscow and the United States too: the Occupy Wall Street Movement, with an encampment a stone's throw from the Wilson Center, has etched references to the "99 percent" into the harsh rhetoric of the 2012 election cycle.

Robin Wright is one of the few American journalists who could compile a volume like this. She understands the region's different cultures, climates, and constituencies—and her book *Rock the Casbah* was the first to recognize the moderate voices that became central to the movement against violent regimes engaged in acts of wanton terror. And Robin's *Iran Primer*, produced by the United States Institute of Peace, remains the go-to work. But there is more to the story.

The Islamists Are Coming: Who They Really Are is about the rest of the story. By bringing together a dozen of the world's experts on Islamist movements, it offers a thoughtful overview of the new order taking shape in the region and will provide needed help to Congress, which continues to lack nuanced understanding of Islam, and provide policymakers in the United States and around the world with a better appreciation of the complexity of change under way.

A few things are already clear. First, the United States has far less influence now than in the past, as does virtually every government in the region. Second, the Arab Awakening has been bottom-up, and the voices of the street cannot be silenced. As a Wilson scholar said recently, "This is the birth of the

Arab citizen." And, third, each country has unique circumstances and culture. One size does not fit all.

Arab voters are identifying with politicians and leaders who tap into their needs—jobs, education, and justice—and provide a way forward. The United States should recalibrate its relationship with the region by adopting a similar approach. Efforts to help countries build political capacity merit strong support.

That means encouraging the very things people fought for from Tunis to Tahrir Square, allowing opposition parties to develop, permitting full and equal participation by women and minorities in the political process, and establishing the checks and balances that ensure dictators can never return. The participation of Islamist parties in fair elections is a nightmare for al Qaeda and its affiliates, which have been largely bypassed in this process.

Islamist political parties have won pluralities or majorities in elections in Tunisia and Egypt. Now they must govern, and their success will be measured by the people who took to the streets by the millions. There should be no rush to judgment.

The road ahead is fraught with obstacles, and the future of Islam as a political force is far from clear. But make no mistake: the Islamists are coming, and we should help to shape the opportunities that presents.

Jane Harman
Director, President, and CEO
Woodrow Wilson International Center for Scholars

March 2012

Abbreviations

AIS	Islamic Salvation Army (Algeria)
AKP	Justice and Development Party (Turkey)
EU	European Union
FIS	Islamic Salvation Front (Algeria)
FJD	Justice and Development Front (Algeria)
GIA	Armed Islamic Group (Algeria)
GSPC	Group for Preaching and Combat (Algeria)
IAF	Islamic Action Front (Jordan)
IIP	Iraqi Islamic Party
ISCI	Islamic Supreme Council of Iraq
LIFG	Libyan Islamic Fighting Group
MIA	Armed Islamic Movement (Algeria)
MJD	Movement for Justice and Development (Syria)
MSP	Movement of Society for Peace (Algeria)
MTI	Islamic Tendency Movement (Tunisia)
MUR	Movement of Unity and Reform (Morocco)
NATO	North Atlantic Treaty Organization
PA	Palestinian Authority
PJD	Justice and Development Party (Morocco)
PLO	Palestine Liberation Organization
SCAF	Supreme Council of the Armed Forces (Egypt)

CHAPTER 1

The Middle East: They've Arrived

Robin Wright

The Islamists are not only coming. In several countries, they've already arrived. Others are primed to take prominent roles down the road. Altogether, Islamist movements are today the most dynamic political force across the Arab world—and they may well be for the next decade or longer.

Their rise to power happened quite abruptly. Within a single year, a rippling wave of uprisings opened political space for Muslim movements that had struggled for decades—in one case, almost a century—just to get in the door. Many of their leaders had spent their careers simply trying to stay out of jail.

But by 2012, more than fifty Islamist parties or movements had mobilized tens of millions of supporters in a dozen Arab countries. They won the right to form governments in Egypt, Tunisia, and Morocco. Others looked set to do well in Yemen and Libya—and potentially in Syria too. Those six countries alone account for more than half of the Arab world's 300 million people.

None of the Islamists were ready to rule, however. Most were as surprised as the ruling autocrats at the speed and breadth of the uprisings. The Islamists joined in initially to avoid being excluded or marginalized. They have been scrambling ever since to develop practical plans to govern. None had specific blueprints.

"It's been an extreme crash course for us," Muslim Brotherhood foreign policy adviser Essam al Haddad told *The Wall Street Journal* a month after Egypt's 2012 parliamentary election. "Remember, for 60 years we were working underground and now we've come out into the light and are staring directly into the sun. We're all blinking and rubbing our eyes, like the Chilean miners. To adapt to this takes time, and we don't have time."

As Islamist parties prove their popularity at the polls, they are becoming both more assertive and more ambitious. Many exhibit a heady arrogance, assuming a hard-earned right to shape the new order. Their rise to power is, in turn, unsettling for both secular groups at home and an outside world that still associates Islamism of any shade with extremism. The tectonic political shake-up will certainly make the future all the more unpredictable.

Yet democratic politics and piety are not necessarily contradictions. Many Islamists have evolved significantly from their early days. In the 1970s and 1980s, the code word to describe them all was *fundamentalist*. Some still fit that label, if in slightly modified forms. But Islamism is not always extremism. In the early twenty-first century, Islamism also has many shades. Several movements today are carving out new niches in diverse forms of *civic Islam*. The lexicon is shifting as politics evolve.

As of 2012, the growing array of Islamist political parties constitute a whole new bloc—separate from the purely militant movements. The distinctions are often nuanced but pivotal in understanding Islamism in the second decade of the twenty-first century. The groups today share at least four common denominators.

First, most political parties do not now embrace theocratic rule, even as they push strong Islamic agendas or values. None are moderate in any Western sense, although a few are progressive in an Islamist context.

For most parties, there are no political templates. Iran's Shiite Islamic republic is not a model, nor is the Sunni religious monarchy of Saudi Arabia—even for groups that have taken aid or inspiration from either. And whatever the rhetoric, re-creating the caliphate or restoring the purity of life from the Prophet Mohammed's time in the seventh century is not what they are really after.

Turkey and Malaysia are more attractive as models to emulate, although partly for their economic prowess and international ties. Despite its ultraconservative Salafi values, Egypt's Nour Party cited Brazil as a model and praised President Luiz Lula da Silva, a socialist, specifically for making Brazil one of the world's top ten economies. "We want to copy the Brazilian experiment here," said Nour spokesman Nader Bakkar. "We want to push small and medium-size enterprises too."

Islamist parties have instead begun—with the emphasis on *begun*—to adapt to twenty-first-century realities, even if sometimes naively or clumsily. Many are struggling to figure out how to create jobs and pick up the garbage with the same fervor that they once simplistically preached "Islam is the solution" to virtually any issue.

Second, most of the fifty parties now engaged in politics have renounced terrorist tactics. Sunni Hamas in the Palestinian territories and Shiite Hezbollah in Lebanon—both having competed in democratic elections endorsed by the international community—are critical exceptions. But virtually all Islamist parties condemn the political absolutism of al Qaeda franchises, which Islamists recognize have discredited their faith and made life more difficult for the faithful. Indeed, militants have murdered far more Muslims than Westerners.

Many parties still use scathing language about Israel that is unacceptable to the international community. Most support the Palestinians in one or more forms of "resistance" against Israel. But most leaders and followers also oppose another war with Israel or terrorist tactics against members of any faith. After Egypt's 2012 election, the two winning Islamist parties pledged to maintain all of Cairo's international treaties. The decision was a stark contrast to the 1981 assassination of Egyptian President Anwar Sadat by Islamic militants after he signed the first peace treaty with Israel.

Third, political Islam is today defined by an increasingly wide spectrum. And no one vision dominates. Indeed, the Islamists' diversity—when the strictly observant believe in only one true path to God—is striking. Goals vary widely. Indeed, the Islamists rarely speak with one voice even within movements.

Some parties, notably in Egypt, are actually rivals. Together, two Islamic parties won some 70 percent of seats in parliament in 2012—and then began to snipe at each other. Conservative Muslim Brotherhood officials described their Salafi rivals as inexperienced and extreme, while members of the ultra-conservative Salafi Party said that the Brothers had compromised their Islamic principles.

Islamist parties have even demonstrated willingness to work with secular and centrist parties, some as partners. After winning a plurality with 41 percent of the popular vote, Tunisia's Ennahda party opted to form a new government with two secular parties. In one of the oddest alliances, Hezbollah formed a coalition with a right-wing Christian party in 2006 that still existed in Lebanon six years later. Whether to widen their power base or ease suspicions, some Islamist parties have demonstrated that they are not going to do what has been done unto them—at least for now.

Fourth and finally, Islamist groups are under pressure to give priority to reality over religion in the early twenty-first century. The same demographics that contributed to street protests against geriatric autocrats—over 60 percent of the Arab world's 300 million people are under the age of thirty—are also fueling internal challenges to geriatric Islamist leaders.

The younger generation often does not buy into intolerant, inflexible, or impractical positions. In some cases, as in Egypt's Muslim Brotherhood, key players have split. Islamist parties face further fractures if they don't address the challenges of daily existence.

Dire economic realities have also forced a sobering, if sometimes reluctant, pragmatism. As Egypt's transition began in 2011, a Gallup poll found that 54 percent of Egyptians listed jobs and economic development as their top priorities. Fewer than 1 percent of Egyptians named implementing Islamic law as their top priority. The results were similar regardless of party affiliation.

A month after winning more than 45 percent of seats in parliament, Egypt's Muslim Brotherhood approved in principle a proposal to borrow $3.2 billion U.S. from the International Monetary Fund. The decision was a flip-flop for the Brotherhood after years of criticizing the West and distancing itself from Western institutions. The decision reflected recognition that ideological purity was a luxury the group could not afford—again, at least for now. "All of a sudden, we found ourselves for the first time, and after a very, very short learning process, asked to take a position that would affect everybody's lives," Haddad told *The Wall Street Journal.*

In the early twenty-first century, the forces of globalization—from trade and tourism to the Internet—also make it tougher for Islamist parties to isolate themselves from the rest of the world. Some parties, notably those in Egypt and Tunisia, could literally not afford to turn totally inward. After winning more than 25 percent of seats in Egypt's parliament in 2012, the Salafi Nour Party proposed creating a new field of medical tourism to make Egypt, again like Brazil, into a center for lower-cost health care—even for Americans.

THE BEGINNING

The modern Islamists have arrived where they are today through four phases. It has not been a straight trajectory. Each phase reflects the scope of change in size, political purpose, priorities, and tactics.

Politicized Islam—Islamism—originally emerged in response to multiple crises in the vacuum created by the Ottoman Empire's collapse and as an alternative to the dominant ideologies of either East or West. Often in the context of European colonialism, Islamist leaders argued that the outside world was out to exploit, control, or destroy Muslim lands. The only way to defend the faith was to fight back, politically, socially, and physically.

Modern Islamism began with a tiny cell in 1928, when a twenty-two-year-old schoolteacher mobilized six disgruntled workers from Egypt's Suez Canal Company. It was originally a social and religious movement. But Hassan al Banna's little group grew into the Muslim Brotherhood, the first popular Islamist movement in the Arab world. It eventually spawned more than eighty branches worldwide.

The Brotherhood created the start-up model that initially focused on fusing Islam with public services, such as schools, clinics, cooperatives, social clubs, welfare providers, and religious support groups. The public services evolved into mini-states-within-states, taking on distinct political agendas for changing the rest of society too. Many other Islamist movements later duplicated the formula.

The first phase peaked in the 1970s, as secular ideologies failed to deliver. The turning point was the 1973 war, when Arabs fought for the first time in the name of Islam. Egypt's attack on Israel was code-named Operation Badr after the Prophet Mohammed's first victory in 623 AD. The Arabs again lost militarily, but they won political goals, including the principle of land for peace. Islam became a winning way to mobilize the public and fight a regional war.

By 1979, Islam also redefined regional politics. Iran's fiery revolution coalesced disparate opposition groups under the banner of Islam. Led by a septuagenarian cleric, the coalition ended dynastic rule dating back more than 2,500 years and then created the world's only modern theocracy. For the first time since the faith was founded fourteen centuries earlier, clerics ruled a state. Islam was suddenly a modern political alternative, too.

The seizure of Saudi Arabia's Grand Mosque by a fundamentalist cell reflected the growing rejection of modernization based on Western ways, which had been the model in many countries since their independence decades earlier. During the two-week takeover, extremists declared the monarchy to be illegitimate. They proclaimed the rule of the Mahdi—the Muslim redeemer—until French forces were brought in to help retake Islam's holiest shrine.

The drama led regimes across the region to redefine modernization in more Islamic terms. Shaken to the core, Saudi Arabia's monarchy ceded greater ground to Wahhabi clerics. Even strictly secular regimes reacted. Under President Sadat, Egypt altered its constitution to ensure that Sharia, or Islamic law, was the basis of all legislation.

The second phase played out in the 1980s. It witnessed the rise of suicide extremism and mass violence. The trend started among Shiites, for whom martyrdom has been a central tenet for fourteen centuries. It soon spread to Sunni militants, for whom it was not a long-held belief. The violent tactics by religious extremists began to redefine modern warfare.

The embryonic cells of Lebanon's Hezbollah initiated suicide bombings with attacks on American and Israeli targets in the early 1980s. As of early 2012, the largest single loss of U.S. military lives since World War II was still the Hezbollah bombing of the Marine peacekeepers' barracks in October 1983 that killed 241. Two American embassies in Beirut were also destroyed, as were several military facilities of the occupying Israeli Defense Forces.

Among Sunnis, two militant movements seized the headlines away from the Palestinian Liberation Organization, an umbrella group for several secular factions. Islamic Jihad was launched in the early 1980s. Its manifesto called for elimination of the "Zionist entity" and creation of a Palestinian state governed by Islamic law. It dispatched dozens of human bombs against Israeli soldiers as well as civilians. Hamas emerged in 1987 during the grassroots uprising known as the *Intifada*, literally the "shaking off." Hamas, too, soon started dispatching suicide warriors.

Throughout the 1980s, thousands of Sunnis from all twenty-two Arab nations also poured into South Asia to challenge the Soviet Union's occupation of Afghanistan. It was the first modern militant jihad. Many of these militant Arabs, including Osama bin Laden, later took their skills and passions home to launch local jihads.

In all three cases, militant groups justified violence as a response to intervention by outside armies or occupation by foreign powers. Again, from their perspective, violence was a reaction. The 1980s was a particularly deadly decade.

The third phase was marked by the rise of Islamist political parties in the 1990s. The emphasis shifted from the bullet to the ballot—or a combination of the two. Islamists began running within political systems, no longer simply sabotaging them from the outside. In the process, Islamists had to move beyond simplistic slogans to develop multi-issue action agendas.

Algeria was the trailblazer in 1991, as the Islamic Salvation Front began to beat more than fifty parties in the Arab world's first fully democratic election. The Front was seen as a party of doers, in contrast to the corrupt and lethargic party that had ruled since independence three decades earlier. The experiment was derailed before the final runoff in 1992, when the Algerian army seized power. Backed by tanks on the streets of Algiers, the new junta nullified the vote, outlawed the Front, and imprisoned its leaders. An underground militant faction, the Armed Islamic Group, soon launched attacks on government targets. Over the next decade, more than 100,000 Algerians died in a civil war between the military regime and extremists.

Yet Islamic parties elsewhere continued the experiment, further spurred by two global shifts: The Cold War's end altered the balance of power in the Middle East—and political calculations in the process. The first wave of democratic elections elsewhere—which empowered hundreds of millions of people, from Russia to Romania and from South Africa to Chile—inspired pursuit of individual empowerment.

In 1992, after a decade underground, Hezbollah's Hassan Nasrallah led the Shiite party into Lebanese elections. Egypt's Muslim Brotherhood ran for parliament in 1995, after a decade of competing under cover of other political parties. Jordan's Islamic Action Front became the largest opposition party elected to parliament. From scenic Morocco and sleepy Kuwait to teeming Yemen, Islamist parties captured the imagination of many voters.

The fourth phase began after al Qaeda's attacks on September 11, 2001, which were as traumatic for many Muslims half a world away as for Americans who witnessed attacks on the World Trade Center and the Pentagon. In the Arab world, hundreds of millions found themselves tainted by a man and a movement they neither knew nor supported.

Muslims were also increasingly victimized, as extremists expanded their suicide attacks from Morocco on the Atlantic to Saudi Arabia on the Persian Gulf. Almost 3,000 people died on 9/11, but militants killed more than 10,000 of their brethren in suicide bombings and other attacks over the next decade. The extremist strategy backfired. In Arab eyes, the many forms of militancy proved costly, unproductive, and ultimately unappealing.

"Every mother in Saudi Arabia or any other Gulf country wants her son or daughter to carry a laptop rather than a rifle or a dagger," reflected Khaled al Maeena, editor of *Arab News*, in Saudi Arabia in 2009. "The appeal of death and destruction doesn't carry much significance anymore because the jihadis have failed to provide anything constructive."

During the first decade of the twenty-first century, the Arab response was a kind of counterjihad—a rejection of extremist movements and tactics to achieve political goals. The response took many tangible forms. But among the most imaginative were the Islamist debates on university campuses, within civil society, among exiles, and even among jailed Islamists about the most effective means of change. The so-called prison debates—notably in Egypt and Libya—eventually led Egypt's Islamic Group (al Gamaa al Islamiyya) to renounce violence in 2002 and the Libyan Islamic Fighting Group to reject terrorism in 2006. A string of public opinion polls since 2007 has tracked the steady decline in support for destructive jihad.

Key clerics also shifted positions. On the 9/11 anniversary in 2007, Sheikh Salman al Oudah, a Saudi cleric who had long been bin Laden's earliest role model, wrote an open letter denouncing the al Qaeda chief. "How many innocent people, children, elderly, and women have been killed, maimed, or banished in the name of al Qaeda?" he wrote. "Will you be happy to meet God almighty carrying the burden of these hundreds of thousands, if not millions, of innocent people on your back?"

A NEW PHASE

In 2011, the raucous Arab uprisings began a new phase. It was launched by unprecedented displays of peaceful civil disobedience in the world's most volatile region. Earlier phases were often a reaction to repressive regimes, regional conflicts, or foreign intervention. The new phase has more of a proactive mission.

This fifth phase is defined by two forces that to the outside world often seem contradictory: democracy and Islam. Polls in 2011 uniformly showed that the majority of Arabs wanted a greater say in their political life. The quest was framed more often as one for "social justice" and "dignity"—local catchphrases for self-determination, political participation, free speech, accountability, and equitable justice—than as a quest for liberal democracy.

But in postuprising countries, public opinion surveys also uniformly found that the majority favored parties that were shaped either moderately or strongly by Islamic values. The shift does not necessarily mean strict Islam as the only organizing principle of life, politics, education, social mores, and dress. Each country or culture has its own dynamics and issues. The shift can also mean reform in a conservative package.

The polls indicate that the election of Islamist parties reflects a shift extending beyond the devout. Many Arabs now want to use their faith as a means to an end, rather than as an end in itself—or as a way to find answers rather than being the answer itself. Politically, Islam offers a comfortable space and legitimacy to search for solutions compatible with global trends. It is no longer about creating an ideal Islamic state. It is more about synthesizing Koranic values with ways of twenty-first-century life spawned by the Internet, Facebook, and satellite television.

The outside world views the shift as a drift toward Islamism. But many within the region instead see the Islamists being pulled toward democracy.

"The theocrats—represented by the Muslim Brotherhood and the Salafists—now dominate a liberating political environment. In the process they are being democratized," said Egyptian political scientist Saad Eddin Ibrahim, who witnessed the prison debates while he was jailed for three years by the Mubarak regime.

"These are people dominated by an ideology that once said democracy was repugnant because it was a Western import. And now not only have they accepted it, but they are riding it and enjoying it. And in so doing—although they won't admit it to you—they are legitimizing democracy in Egypt and, in turn, with Egypt as its intellectual center, the Arab world too," Ibrahim explained. "Visiting Egypt a year from now, I doubt if you will find the lifestyle of Egyptians has changed. Politics yes, government maybe. But it's much more difficult to change society."

THE NEW SPECTRUM

In the latest phase, Islamists are not "one size fits all." Indeed, the new spectrum is something of a labyrinth in the early twenty-first century. But the parties generally break down into three broad categories, say Egyptian experts Ismail Alexandrani and Dina Shehata.

The first and most basic category is classical Islamism. Its goal is to implement Islamic law, or Sharia. Its political face focuses on ensuring that the government complies with fixed scriptures or texts. Classical Islamists demonstrate little adaptability. They trust clerics and religious scholars to speak and act on behalf of the people.

Classical Islamists can differ by sect, however, because of the disparate powers of their respective clerics. As a result, pure Islamism among Shiites is more likely to produce theocratic rule. Among Sunnis, pure Islamism is more likely to produce authoritarian rule, but not a theocracy. The difference dates back to the original schism within Islam in the seventh century over leadership and politics.

In Shiite Islam, the clerics are empowered to interpret God's word to the faithful. As in Catholicism, the clergy has absolute power, which in Iran was translated into political power too after the 1979 revolution. The clerics now literally rule. Classical Shiite Islamism also considers the citizen to have responsibilities and duties, but not rights. Iranian revolutionary leader Ayatollah Khomeini epitomized the classical Shiite Islamist.

In Sunni Islam, the clerics are only advisers to the faithful. So in Sunni Islamist societies, clerics are unlikely to become the rulers. Instead, Islamist leaders are more likely to be secular politicians who want to implement Islamic law, often with a singular vision. Classical Sunni Islamism has a ceiling on rights that is based on what is allowed in Islam, which would preclude alcohol, pornography, and homosexuality. The writings of Egyptian thinker Sayyid Qutb reflect the classical Sunni Islamism.

The Salafis are also classical Islamists. But they have their own subsections, again reflecting the Islamist maze. Among them are the following: The traditional or scholarly Salafis are basically "schools" gathered around specific clerics. The scientific Salafis are focused on learning Sharia but not on going into politics, except that they tend to vote as a bloc. The Costa Salafis, named after a chain of Cairo coffee shops where they tend to hang out, are from a younger generation. They do not necessarily take orders from their ultraconservative sheikhs and do share many of the original Tahrir protesters' demands for political openings. The ex-jihadi Salafis include former extremists who have renounced violence and are largely in the Salafi political camp now.

The second broader category is neo-Islamism. Its members are more flexible, informed, and mature in their political outlook. For them, Sharia is about values, civilization, and political context. Neo-Islamists are seeking the ultimate objectives of Sharia but without bonding each situation to a certain religious text. They believe that Islam is dynamic and not a set of fixed rules and tenets, but rather an organic belief system that can adapt to or live with the times. Neo-Islamists can be progressive and, on some issues, even liberal. Neo-Islamists trust the reform scholars.

The Muslim Brotherhood has begun to move from classical Islamism to neo-Islamism, the two Egyptian experts contend. But the Brothers also have their own internal factions, each of which tugs the movement in a different direction. The conservative faction has unquestioning fealty to the organization and its dictates. The nationalist faction defines its agenda on the basis of the public interests of all Egyptians. And the neo-liberal faction, which is reflected in an emerging business elite, envisions the spread of Islamist goals through development or economic renaissance.

But the Brothers also have up to twenty different trends within the movement, according to Khaled Hanafy, a member of parliament and an ophthalmologist. "We share great principles, and within those principles we respect the differences," he said. "We differ on education, culture, and the economic state. I even differ from my wife, who also ran for parliament. It is very good for the organization to have differences."

The Brotherhood remains largely in the classical camp, however, because it invokes tight discipline over its members after deliberations. "When we decide, there is one opinion," Hanafy added. "The majority decide, then the minority should obey."

The third broader category is post-Islamism. Its adherents separate religious and political discourse, although they do not divorce values from politics. They would not, for example, embrace classical secularism. They do not publicly propagate Sharia, but as individuals they may be committed Muslims and consider ethics to be pivotal in political life.

Post-Islamists also believe that the people are the origin of political authority and power. They recognize the people's responsibility for their choices. Post-Islamists remove the ceiling on rights, which are no longer limited by religious texts. And they trust people's religious consciousness—without needing to rely on clerics or scholars. Turkey's Justice and Development Party is the best example of post-Islamism.

THE FUTURE

The next decade will almost certainly be far more traumatic for both insiders and outsiders than the past decade, although often because of economic challenges as much as the new politics. Pity the inheritors of the Arab world's broken political and economic systems, whoever they are.

Officials in elected Islamist governments have gradually acknowledged their naïve illusions about ruling. Mustapha Kamel Nabli, the governor of the Tunisian central bank, told the 2012 World Economic Forum in Davos, "One year ago, when the revolution started, I think we were dreaming, and we were dreaming with our feet in the sky. Now we are still dreaming, but we are dreaming with our feet on the ground."

Political Goals

Despite stunning electoral endorsements, however, most individual Islamist parties had won only pluralities by early 2012. Only Hamas won an outright majority in the 2006 Palestinian vote. (Egypt's Muslim Brotherhood held back from running for the presidency or for all parliamentary seats in 2012.) Like parties of any ilk, Islamist parties will eventually want the majority.

Their next target may be municipal polls to deepen their hold. And the more power they accrue—like parties of any ilk—the less likely will be their need to compromise with others and the greater will be the danger of single-minded or narrow-minded rule.

Unity

At the same time, however, Islamist groups may also fragment further. Their spectrum may keep expanding as a result of either demographics or ideas. They already have different visions. For some, Islam offers values by which to define goals. For others, particularly for Salafis, Islam is the framework for all ways of life, public and private. Those fundamental differences may translate into specific flashpoints as parties sit down to write new constitutions, notably on provisions about how rigorously Islam's social mores and penal code are implemented.

Diverse Islamist parties also cater to disparate segments of society. In Egypt, the Muslim Brotherhood's base draws significantly from the urban, the educated, and the professional classes, and from the middle and lower-middle classes. The Brotherhood has a sophisticated organization. Its members must pass standards and have references. And after eight decades, it has a mature understanding of Egyptian politics. In the 2005 elections, the Brotherhood won eighty-eight seats in parliament during Hosni Mubarak's rule, making it the largest opposition party. For years, its members dominated Egypt's professional unions, including syndicates for doctors and engineers.

By contrast, Egypt's Salafi newcomers tend to be less educated and far more traditional. Their stronghold is in Alexandria and the Delta, with large pockets in greater Cairo. Because they renounced political life until after the 2011 uprising, they are poorly organized. Their Nour Party is little more than an assemblage of followers of diverse sheikhs. They are far more committed to social or lifestyle aspects of Sharia, or Islamic law. They are often impractical about solutions on big issues such as the economy.

Women's Rights

Under Islamist regimes, women are unlikely to see many short-term benefits—and quite possibly could face serious setbacks. Women have been at the forefront of uprisings in every country. But few Islamist parties have enlightened or forward-leaning policies to promote gender equality. In Egypt, the Brotherhood has an active Sisterhood of female members, but it resists the idea of a female president.

The Salafis even refused to allow female candidates—mandated by election laws—to use their pictures in the campaign or on ballots. They also favor separation of the sexes. "We want segregation in school and in public and in the workplace so people can concentrate," said Sheikh Mohammed Kurdy, a member of parliament from Egypt's Nour Party. He has two wives and ten children.

The Economy

On the economy, most Islamists favor a balance between free markets and so-called social justice, which means more equitable distribution of resources long hoarded by autocratic regimes. Their policies stem from their service-oriented histories and mass grassroots support, as well as from their own experiences in small businesses or the professions.

"I would like to ask the businessmen in the room. Have you suffered from the victory of the Islamists? You supported the dictatorships in the past," Moroccan Prime Minister Abdelilah Benkirane told the 2012 World Economic Forum in Davos. "Today we can guarantee your interests more than they did in the past."

Foreign Policy

Relations between Islamist parties and the outside world will often be uneasy. The harder the party's line, the harder their relations will be with others. The relationships could get quite tense. The two sides fundamentally view the political shift through different prisms. To the outside world, Islamists are pushing aside democrats, liberals, and secular politicians. To Islamists, democracy has prevailed after decades or centuries of autocratic rule.

"I do not believe the new regimes should be called political Islamist regimes. We must be careful with our terminology," Tunisian Prime Minister Hamadi Jebali told the 2012 World Economic Forum in Davos. "For the first time in the Arab world, we have free and honest elections that led to democratic regimes."

Aid

Across the board, Islamists want to cut back both foreign influence and foreign aid. Many believe that the colonial era has not yet really ended. But some also show a realism about diplomatic ties and aid.

"We want Egyptians to have a dignified life," said Brotherhood foreign affairs spokesman Khalez Kazzaz. "One-third lives in poverty. One-third is illiterate. This means in the short term that we have to maintain and then strengthen our international relations. Long term we want to be less dependent. We are not in a phase where we will remove the plug of some of the funding. We need more funding. Our bigger priority is economic development."

Pace of Change

Despite the breathtaking first year of political change, some Islamists indicated that they may not push for instant implementation of Sharia, especially its most controversial aspects.

"We all know there are some commands in Islam—for example, if you steal, your hand should be cut off," said Sheikh Mohammed Kurdy, a Salafi member of parliament from Egypt's Nour Party. "But we may delay some of it for now because of conditions in the country. We can't do it until everyone will have a place to live, food to eat, a job. They should not be thinking of stealing then because they won't need to steal."

Yet political Islam is also, for now, a driving force in the new order. "Without Islam, we will not have any real progress," explained Diaa Rashwan of Cairo's Al Ahram Center for Political and Strategic Studies.

"If we go back to the European Renaissance, it was based on Greek and Roman philosophy and heritage. When Western countries built their own progress, they didn't go out of their epistemological or cultural history. Japan is still living in the culture of the Samurai, but in a modern way. The Chinese are still living the traditions created by Confucianism. Their version of communism is certainly not Russian.

"So why," he mused, "do we have to go out of our history?"

Robin Wright is a joint fellow at the Woodrow Wilson International Center for Scholars and the U.S. Institute of Peace. A former correspondent for The Washington Post, *her most recent book is* Rock the Casbah: Rage and Rebellion Across the Islamic World (2011). *Her blog is http://robinwrightblog.blogspot. com and her book website is http://www.robinwright.net.*

CHAPTER 2

Islam: The Democracy Dilemma

Olivier Roy

The long-standing debate about Islam and democracy has reached a stunning turning point. Since the Arab uprisings began in late 2010, political Islam and democracy have become increasingly interdependent. The debate over whether they are compatible is now virtually obsolete. Neither can now survive without the other.

In countries undergoing transitions, the only way for Islamists to maintain their legitimacy now is through elections. Their own political culture may still not be democratic. But they are now defined by the new political landscape and have been forced, in turn, to redefine themselves, much as the Roman Catholic Church ended up accepting democratic institutions even as its own practices remained oligarchic.

At the same time, there will be no institutionalization of democracy for Arab countries in transition without including mainstream Islamist groups, such as the Muslim Brotherhood in Egypt, Ennahda in Tunisia, or Islah in Yemen. The so-called Arab Spring cleared the way for the Islamists. And even if many Islamists do not share the democratic culture of the demonstrators, the Islamists have to take into account the new playing field the demonstrations created.

The debate over Islam and democracy used to be a chicken-and-egg issue: which came first? Democracy has certainly not been at the core of Islamist ideology. Egypt's Muslim Brotherhood has historically been strictly centralized and obedient to a supreme leader who rules for life. And Islam has certainly not been factored into promotion of secular democracy. Indeed, skeptics have long argued that the two forces were allegoric or even anathema to each other.

But the outside world wrongly assumed that Islam would first have to experience a religious reformation before its followers could embark on political democratization—replicating the Christian experience when the Reformation gave birth to the Enlightenment and then to modern democracy. In fact, however, liberal Muslim intellectuals had little influence in either inspiring or directing the Arab uprisings. The original protesters in Cairo's Tahrir Square referred to democracy as a universal concept—and not to any sort of Islamic democracy.

The development of both political Islam and democracy now appear to go hand in hand, albeit not at the same pace. The new political scene is transforming the Islamists as much as the Islamists are transforming the political scene.

Today the compatibility between Islam and democracy does not center on theological issues, but rather on the concrete way in which believers recast their faith in a rapidly changing political environment. Whether liberal or fundamentalist, the new forms of religiosity are individualistic and more in tune with the democratic ethos.

THE BEGINNING

Democratization was first raised as an issue in the Middle East in the late nineteenth and early twentieth centuries. The initial debate centered mainly on modernization of the state—meaning secularization of the state, specifically as the basis for law and selection of leaders. The collapse of the Ottoman Empire's caliphate after World War I, which created many of the modern Arab states, gave urgency to the issue of modern governance. Additional pressures to modernize and secularize came from outside the Arab world. They played out during European colonial rule in the Arab world.

As Arab countries gained independence, mostly between the 1940s and 1960s, the outside world assumed that the transition to democracy would rely on an enlightened authoritarian leader who could facilitate democratization but also serve as a bulwark against Islamic fundamentalism. The role was embodied by Kemal Atatürk, who created modern Turkey out of the ashes of the Ottoman Empire.

Islamists responded by arguing that their religion was an all-encompassing system that could solve any political, economic, or social problem raised by modernization. Early Islamists did not totally dismiss democracy as irrelevant. They often pointed to a central tenet of the faith—the *shura* or advisory council, where ideas were debated before submitting proposals to the *amir*, or leader. The shura was also empowered to elect the amir, although the amir's position was held for life and was basically without any checks or balances.

THE EVOLUTION

When Islamism gained ground during the 1970s and 1980s, it was initially dominated by revolutionary movements and radical tactics. Over the next thirty years, however, the religious revival in Arab societies diversified. Movements took on individual identities and goals. Social shifts also reined in radicalism. The toll of death and destruction also diverted interest away from militancy.

Even the proliferation of media outside state control played a role. In the mid-1990s, al Jazeera became the first independent satellite television station. Within a generation, there were more than 500 stations. Many offered a wide range of religious programming—with hosts ranging from traditional sheikhs to liberal Muslims—which in turn introduced the idea of diversity. Suddenly, there was no single truth in a religion that had preached one path to God for fourteen centuries. *Islam* literally means submission, as in submission to God.

Islamists also changed through both victory and defeat—or a combination of the two. Shiite Islamists won a political victory in Iran's 1979 revolution. But three decades later, the world's only modern theocracy was increasingly ostracized by the world, leading many Islamists to ask, "What went wrong?"

In Algeria, Sunni Islamists were pushed aside in a military coup on the eve of an election victory in 1992. The party was banned, and its leaders imprisoned. A more militant faction then took on the military, and more than 100,000 people were killed in a decade-long civil war. The bloody aftermath of the Arab world's first democratic election had a rippling effect on the calculations of Islamist groups across the region.

As a result of their experience, Islamists increasingly compromised to get into or stay in the political game. In Egypt, the Muslim Brothers ran for parliament whenever allowed, often by making tactical alliances with secular parties. In Kuwait and Morocco, Islamists abided by the political rules whenever they ran for parliament, even when it meant embracing monarchies that contradicted their own ideologies. Morocco's Justice and Development Party recognized the sacred dimension of the king so that it could participate in elections, and Jordan's Muslim Brotherhood publicly supported the king despite growing discontent among the Arab Bedouin tribes.

A generation of Islamic activists forced into exile also played a major role in redirecting their movements. Most leaders or members ended up spending more time in Western countries than in Islamic nations—and, notably, not in Saudi Arabia and Iran. In the West, the Islamists came into contact with other secular and liberal dissidents as well as nongovernment organizations, such as Human Rights Watch, Amnesty International, and Freedom House, that facilitated the flow of ideas.

In the 1990s, exiled activists increasingly framed their agendas in terms of democracy and human rights. They acknowledged that simplistic slogans such as "Islam is the solution" were not enough to build programs or coalitions capable of removing dictators. Rachid al Ghannouchi, cofounder of Tunisia's Ennahda Party, concluded almost twenty years before the Arab uprisings that democracy was a better tool to fight dictatorships than the call for either jihad or Sharia.

THE SOCIAL REVOLUTION

Islamists have changed because society has changed too. The rise of Islamists has reflected the social and cultural revolutions as much as a political revolution.

A new generation has entered the political space, especially in the major cities. It is the generation of Tahrir Square, the epicenter of Egypt's uprising against Hosni Mubarak. When the uprisings began, two-thirds of the Arab world's 300 million people were under the age of thirty. The young are better educated and more connected with the outside world than any previous generation. Many speak or understand a foreign language. The females are often as ambitious as their male counterparts. Both genders eagerly question and debate. Most of the young are able to identify and even shrug off propaganda.

The Arab baby boom generation also does not share the patriarchal culture of its elders, and the majority of baby boomers reject patronizing dictators. Many are attracted more to ideas of good governance and freedom than to charismatic leaders. The shift does not necessarily mean that baby boomers are more liberal or more secular than their parents. Many Arab baby boomers are attracted by new forms of religiosity that stress individual choice, direct relations with God, self-realization, and self-esteem. But even when they join Islamic movements, they bring along their critical approach and reluctance to blindly follow an aging leadership.

The transformation is visible even among young Salafis in Egypt. They may wear baggy trousers and long, white shirts, imitating the Prophet Mohammed and leading the outside world to question their willingness to modernize. But they also often wear shiny sunglasses and sport shoes. They are part of a global culture.

For decades, the Salafis opposed participation in politics. But after the uprisings, they completely reversed course. They jumped into politics, hastily registering as political parties. At universities, clubs of young Salafis—including females—have joined public debate forums.

The influence of the current baby boom generation will be enduring. Their numbers are likely to dominate politics for much of their lives—potentially another thirty to forty years—because the fertility rate has plummeted almost everywhere in the Arab world since their birth.

REGIONAL AND GLOBAL FACTORS

Broader geostrategic changes, both global and regional, also affected the Islamist movements and ultimately prevented the religious revival from returning to rigid traditions. In the 1970s and 1980s, Islamism emerged at the height of the Cold War between the Soviet bloc and the West. The Soviet Union's collapse in 1991 ended the Cold War and altered the bipolar balance of power worldwide. Elections and democracy came increasingly into vogue.

Islamist leaders—such as Iranian revolutionary leader Ayatollah Ruhollah Khomeini—claimed to offer a third way between communism and capitalism. But by the 1990s, no country—either Sunni or Shiite—served as a beacon for Islamists. The luster had clearly faded from Iran's 1979 revolution. Sunnis resented Tehran's efforts to export its Shiite ideology. But

Sunni Islamists were also critical of the royal family in Saudi Arabia, the only country where Sharia is the sole law of the land. The distrust was reciprocated. The Muslim Brothers, many of whom did not oppose Iraqi President Saddam Hussein after his 1990 invasion of Kuwait, were not allowed in Saudi Arabia.

In the 1990s, progress in the peace process also changed the political landscape. The 1993 Oslo Accords did not end the Israeli-Palestinian conflict. But the peace agreement transformed the Palestine Liberation Organization and chairman Yasser Arafat from international terrorists into legitimate interlocutors. And the agreement proved that a political process might be more productive than armed violence. Even Hamas, the Palestinian Islamist movement that rejected the peace process, was eventually dragged into politics and, in 2006, into competing at the ballot box.

Ironically, Islamist groups also occasionally found themselves on the same side as the West. They both sided with the Mujahideen after the Soviet Union's invasion of Afghanistan in the 1980s. They both backed Muslim rights in Bosnia and Chechnya in the 1990s.

After the 9/11 attacks, Islamists initially benefited from President George W. Bush's call for greater democracy in the Arab world, which briefly led to some openings. In 2005, Egypt amended its constitution to allow multiparty presidential elections. It also allowed the Muslim Brotherhood to field more candidates. The Islamists won eighty-eight seats, making it the country's largest opposition movement. Paradoxically, the U.S. war on terrorism, launched in 2001, also forced Islamist movements to make clearer choices in rejecting terrorism and militant jihad.

The biggest stimulant in the early twenty-first century, however, was the rise of Turkey's Islamists after decades of confrontation with secular parties and the military. Since 2002, Turkey's Justice and Development Party has won three landslide victories. The new model has no explicit Islamic references—and even denies that it is Islamist. The party won by emphasizing economic development (including application for membership in the European Union) and conservative social values.

THE THREE CAMPS

During the debate about Islam and democracy, Muslim religious scholars and intellectuals have fallen into three broad camps.

The first camp rejects both democracy and secularism as Western concepts that are not even worth refuting. In this fundamentalist view, participating even in everyday politics, such as joining a political party or voting, is *haram*, or religiously forbidden. This view has been the position of the Wahhabi clerics in Saudi Arabia, the Taliban in Afghanistan, and—for decades—the various Salafi schools.

The second camp claims that returning to the "true tenets" of Islam will create the best kind of democracy. In this conservative view, the faithful may deliberate to understand the true path, but the idea that religion is the ultimate truth is not negotiable. These Islamists invoke the concept of *towhid*, or the oneness, uniqueness, and sovereignty of God, which can never be replaced by the will of the people.

But the second camp also invokes Muslim practices to claim that modern political ideology meets the basic requirements of democracy. For example, it says the shura, the forum or council for deliberations, is the equivalent of a parliament.

The third camp advocates *ijtihad*, or reinterpreting Islam to make it compatible with the universal concept of democracy. This position is more common among lay intellectuals than among clerics. But opening up the doors of ijtihad, which conservative scholars had believed were closed since the Middle Ages, has already produced its own spectrum of ideas, not all in agreement with each other.

The Islamist reformers often have a larger audience in the West than in their own countries, not just because of domestic censorship and harassment. Some reformers are deemed to be too intellectual, too abstract, or too tied to an artificial theology. Their philosophical approach is disconnected from popular religious practices, and the teachings at most madrassas, or religious schools.

THE FUTURE

The new Islamist brand will increasingly mix technocratic modernism and conservative values. The movements that have entered the political mainstream cannot now afford to turn their backs on multiparty politics for fear of alienating a significant portion of the electorate that wants stability and peace, not revolution.

But in countries undergoing transitions, the Islamists will face a tough balancing act. In Egypt, for example, the Muslim Brotherhood cannot cede its conviction that Islam is all encompassing. Yet the Brotherhood risks losing popular support unless it can also reconcile Islam with good governance and human rights in practice.

To do that, the Muslim Brothers may have to translate Islamic norms into more universal conservative values—such as limiting the sale of alcohol in a way that is closer to Utah's rules than to Saudi laws and promoting "family values" instead of imposing Sharia norms on women. The political debate over the next few years may also concentrate on specific issues, such as censorship related to blasphemy and pornography, and religious freedom under the rubric of apostasy, or the right to leave Islam for another religion or no religion at all.

Within their own movements, many Islamists still do not share the democratic culture of the uprisings. But given their own demographics and the wider constituency they seek, Islamists will increasingly have to take into account the new political playing field created by the demonstrations—even among themselves.

The exercise of power can actually have a debilitating effect on ideological parties. And for all their recent political success, Islamists also face a set of constraints: They do not control the armed forces. Their societies are more educated and sophisticated in their worldviews—and more willing to actively express their opinions. Women are increasingly players, reflected by their numbers in universities.

Ironically, elected Islamists may face opposition from the clergy. Among Sunnis, Islamists usually do not control the religious institutions. Egypt's Muslim Brotherhood does not control Al Azhar University, the Islamic world's oldest educational institution, dating back more than 1,000 years. The Brothers may have won a plurality in parliament, but none of them is authorized to say what is or is not Islamic without being challenged by a wide range of other religious actors, from clerics to university scholars.

The biggest constraint on Islamists, however, may be economic realities. Focusing simply on Sharia will not spawn economic development—and could actually deter foreign investment and tourism. The labor force is outspoken and does not want to be forgotten, but economic globalization requires sensitivity to international pressures too. The newly elected Islamists face political rejection if they do not deliver the economic goods.

After the Arab uprisings, the Islamists will find it harder to play on the Arab-Israeli conflict or tensions with the international community. Israel is still unpopular. And anti-Western xenophobia has visibly grown. But the battle lines in the Middle East are shifting.

As of 2012, the most dangerous divide has more to do with tensions between Sunnis and Shiites. The differences are symbolized by deepening political fault lines between the Sunni religious monarchy in Saudi Arabia and Iran's Shiite theocracy. But the differences ripple across the region, from the tiny archipelago of Bahrain to strategic Syria. Just as Islamism is redefining the region's politics, Islamic politics and sectarian differences are redefining the region's conflicts.

Olivier Roy, a professor at the European University Institute in Florence, is the author of Globalized Islam *(2004) and* Holy Ignorance *(2010). He heads the ReligioWest Research project at http://www.eui.eu/Projects/ReligioWest/About/.*

CHAPTER 3

Egypt: The Founders

Samer Shehata

The single most powerful and prolific Islamist movement was born in Egypt, the intellectual center of the Arab world. Formed in 1928, the Muslim Brotherhood was started as a social and religious club by a twenty-two-year-old schoolteacher, who recruited six members of the Suez Canal Company. It has since become the ideological grandfather of more than eighty-five other Islamist groups in dozens of countries well beyond the Arab world. Members or supporters of its many branches now number in the tens of millions.

More than any other group, the Muslim Brotherhood reflects the way Islamist politics have transformed Arab politics in the early twenty-first century. In the 2011–12 elections, the Brotherhood's political wing, the Freedom and Justice Party, won 43 percent of the seats in parliament in the freest vote in Egypt's 5,000-year history. All together, Islamist parties won about 70 percent of the seats in the People's Assembly, the lower and more powerful house of parliament.

But the Brotherhood has also evolved significantly over the eight decades between its birth and its rise to power. The Brotherhood first tried to run for office in the 1940s but was repeatedly outlawed. It went through a militant phase in the 1950s and 1960s, when some of its members attempted to assassinate political leaders, including President Gamal Abdel Nasser. The regime undertook a massive crackdown against the organization, and thousands of its members were imprisoned and tortured. During this period, the Brotherhood's chief ideologue justified violent jihad. Even after the Brotherhood renounced extremism in the late 1960s, its platform continued to be intolerant of Christians and women's rights. It called for laws to comply with Sharia, or Islamic law. And it rejected Egypt's peace accord with Israel. Under the cover of other parties, it began running candidates for office again in the mid-1980s. In 2005, it won eighty-eight seats in parliament.

The Brotherhood faced regular repression under three successive presidents—Gamal Abdel Nasser, Anwar Sadat, and Hosni Mubarak, who tolerated some of the movement's social welfare services but methodically curtailed political activities. Members and leaders of the Brotherhood were frequently detained and imprisoned, even after it became the largest opposition group in parliament in 2005.

The Egyptian uprising in 2011 caught the Islamists by surprise. But they quickly capitalized on it, mobilizing members and security for Tahrir Square. After Mubarak was forced to step down, the Brotherhood formed a new political party to run for office. After decades of repression, the Brotherhood has gone from being an embattled opposition to the most powerful bloc— holding 216 of 498 seats in a parliament charged with writing Egypt's new constitution. The Brotherhood is now poised to play critical roles as Egypt attempts to make the transition to democracy.

THE BEGINNING

Hassan al Banna founded the Society of Muslim Brothers in the provincial town of Ismailiyya during a tumultuous political period. The son of a cleric, Banna came of age as Egyptians pressed for an end to British occupation and Western cultural and economic encroachment, including Christian missionary activity. Banna believed that Egypt—and the Muslim world in general— were weak and blighted by corruption, social inequality, and foreign exploitation.

Ismailiyya was a microcosm of the challenge. Home to the Suez Canal Company and British military garrisons, the town was filled with luxurious homes for foreigners juxtaposed with poor living conditions for Egyptian workers. Western influence permeated education, language, law, social habits, and values.

Like other Islamic modernists, Banna believed that Muslim societies were weak because they had fallen out of touch with their faith. He held that the key to achieving national independence, progress, and development was an Islamic renewal that restored religion in everyday life and politics, including application of Sharia, or Islamic law.

The Brotherhood began in 1928 as a social welfare society devoted to Islamic revival and social reform. The society built mosques, schools for both boys and girls, youth centers, and Koranic schools. It undertook literacy campaigns. It engaged in many forms of charitable work. It also created small economic enterprises and artisan workshops.

Egypt's first mass social and political movement experienced rapid growth. The Brotherhood had 50 branches nationwide by 1934, expanding to 300 branches with some 50,000 members by 1938. When Banna was assassinated in 1949, the Brotherhood had approximately 2,000 branches with an estimated 500,000 members, making it the largest organized force in the country. It also soon became the mother of all mass Sunni Islamist organizations in the Arab world.

The Brotherhood initially recruited members primarily from the lower-middle class and working class, including employees of the Suez Canal Company. Members also were artisans, laborers, merchants, and civil servants. A charismatic speaker and efficient organizer, Banna preached in villages across the country. The movement's nonelitist character was an important source of its strength. The educated and professional middle classes eventually constituted the backbone of the movement and its leadership.

In the 1930s, the Brotherhood became increasingly involved in politics, taking strong positions on both domestic and regional affairs. It called for immediate evacuation of British forces from Egypt and raised awareness and funds for the 1936 general strike in Palestine. To support its causes, the movement published pamphlets, newsletters, and eventually a weekly newspaper that took up social, cultural, and religious issues. It held regular public meetings, rallies, and national conferences. Banna was a frequent speaker across the country.

The Brotherhood's rapid growth and activities led to Banna's first brief detention in 1941. In 1945, he was one of a handful of Brotherhood candidates who ran for parliament. They all lost in what was widely seen as a flawed poll.

Like other political parties, such as the Wafd, Nationalist, and Young Egypt parties, the Brotherhood established a small clandestine militia in the early 1940s. This era was a period of nationalist agitation, political instability, and occasional violence, including bombings and assassinations. A member of the Nationalist Party assassinated Prime Minister Ahmed Maher Pasha in 1945.

The Brotherhood's militia, known as the "special apparatus," was trained in the use of small arms. It was ostensibly charged with armed resistance against British occupying forces, but it was also involved in several domestic operations. Two members of the group assassinated a prominent judge in 1947 after he sentenced a Muslim Brother to prison for attacks against British soldiers. There are conflicting accounts of how much control Banna had over the militia and whether some actions were taken without his knowledge or orders.

The Brotherhood also supported the war effort in Palestine in 1948 by sending arms and volunteers to the front. In November 1948, the government discovered an arms cache at the home of a Brotherhood leader responsible for aiding the Palestine war effort. Other arrests led to the government's discovery of the movement's militia.

The Egyptian government moved quickly to dissolve the Brotherhood, confiscating its assets and arresting many members, although not Banna. In retaliation, a young Muslim Brother assassinated Prime Minister Al Nuqrashi Pasha on December 28, 1948. Banna denounced the assassination, but less than two months later Banna was assassinated by members of the Egyptian political police.

THE NASSER ERA

On July 23, 1952, a group of junior military officers led by Gamal Abdel Nasser staged a coup to depose King Farouk. The Free Officers Movement promised national independence, social justice, development, and democracy. The Free Officers had previous contact with members of the Brotherhood, including Banna. Some Free Officers, notably a young officer named Anwar Sadat, were sympathetic to the Brotherhood's ideas.

The Brotherhood initially welcomed the revolution, but the honeymoon was brief. The military junta had no interest in partners and did not return to the barracks, as promised. To consolidate its own power, the military began to eliminate rivals, dissolve political parties, and put former senior regime officials on trial. The military also outlawed the Brotherhood and arrested many of its leaders. The military and the Brotherhood then moved into open conflict.

In October 1954, a Brotherhood member attempted to assassinate Nasser during a visit to Alexandria. Over the next decade, thousands of Muslim Brothers were arrested; others went into exile. The crackdown continued until after Nasser's death in 1970.

The 1960s were a particularly dark period for the movement. The Brotherhood was radicalized by Sayyid Qutb, a writer intensely critical of Western civilization, of Egypt under Nasser, and of authoritarian governments in Muslim countries. Qutb was arrested following the 1954 assassination attempt against Nasser and spent a decade in prison.

Qutb's ideas later influenced extremist movements—from Islamic Jihad and the Islamic Group (al Gamaa al Islamiyya) to al Qaeda—that justified violence for political ends. He was released from prison in 1964 but was soon rearrested for allegedly plotting an assassination attempt against Nasser. Qutb was tried and executed in 1966.

After intense internal debates, the Brotherhood moved away from Qutb's ideas, renounced violence, and gave priority to religious propagation rather than to political power. The turning point was marked by the 1969 publication of *Preachers, Not Judges* by Hassan al Hodeiby, the general guide of the movement. Hodeiby rejected *takfir*, the idea of declaring Muslims infidels, and rejected violence as a method of political change.

THE SADAT ERA

The Brotherhood's status shifted under Anwar Sadat, a former army officer who succeeded Nasser in 1970. Sadat released many of the movement's leaders from prison and used the Brotherhood to counterbalance his Nasserist rivals. Although the movement was still legally outlawed, it was permitted to operate on university campuses. Islamists swept student elections between 1975 and 1979, until the government dissolved the student unions. The group was also allowed to propagate its message (*dawa*, or the call) and to reestablish many of its social welfare activities. Religious publications proliferated, and two newspapers associated with the movement began circulation in 1976.

Sadat was also less hostile, if not sympathetic, to some of the movement's ideas. He called himself the "believer president" and employed Islamic rhetoric and symbols to bolster his legitimacy. He also introduced Sharia, or Islamic law, into the Egyptian constitution. Article 2 of the 1971 constitution declared that "the principles of the Sharia are *a* principal source of legislation."(Previous constitutions had only stipulated that Islam was the state religion.) In 1980, Sadat amended the article to stipulate that Sharia was "*the* principal source of legislation."

The 1970s generally witnessed increasing religiosity and conservatism across the Arab world. The 1973 Middle East war was a particularly important turning point. The war, an invasion designed by Sadat to take Israel by surprise, was fought using Islamic symbolism, not Arab nationalism. The Arabs lost militarily, but the war shook Israel, altered the status quo, and encouraged both countries to move toward peace negotiations.

But Sadat personally became increasingly unpopular in the late 1970s. His peace treaty with Israel, including his trip to Jerusalem, was contentious at home and isolated Egypt in the Arab world. Economic conditions deteriorated, resulting in the 1977 bread riots. Sadat's rule gradually became more authoritarian. Radical Islamist movements—such as Takfir wa Hijra, which rejected the Brotherhood's call for reform and instead promoted isolation and radical change through violence—emerged during this period. After Sadat's crackdown on political opponents, members of Islamic Jihad assassinated the Egyptian leader on October 6, 1981, during a parade to commemorate the 1973 war.

THE MUBARAK ERA

During Mubarak's thirty-year rule, the Brotherhood began to participate in formal politics, including elections for parliament, professional syndicates or unions, student councils, and even faculty associations. The Brotherhood so successfully gained control of unions for doctors, pharmacists, engineers, and lawyers that the regime changed the election rules to block the Brothers from dominating those groups.

But the Brotherhood's most strategic decision in the 1980s was to run for parliament even though it was still outlawed. It fielded candidates under cover of other opposition forces. For the 1984 election, the Brotherhood forged a coalition with the Wafd Party. The alliance took slightly more than 15 percent of the vote, or eight seats for the Brotherhood and forty-eight for the Wafd in a 448-person legislature. In the 1987 elections, the Brotherhood allied with the Labor and Ahrar parties. The alliance took 17 percent of the vote for fifty-six seats, thirty-six of which went to the Brothers.

Participating in the democratic process had a profound influence on the movement. It gained practical experience with campaigns, voter mobilization, media outreach, and parliamentary affairs—the processes of democracy. But the experience also deepened the movement's interest in pluralism and forced it to articulate clearer positions and specific solutions to critical issues. Both required compromises.

The Brotherhood was not Egypt's only Islamist movement, however. During the 1990s, radical Islamist cells increased their violent attacks against the Mubarak regime as well as the Coptic Christian minority and foreign tourists, particularly in Upper Egypt. The deadliest terrorist attack was carried out in Luxor, where more than sixty people—mostly foreign tourists—were killed in 1997. Although it had renounced violence, the Brotherhood often paid a price too. After the 1995 assassination attempt against Mubarak in Ethiopia, the regime cracked down on all Islamist groups. Hundreds of the Brotherhood's members were imprisoned; some were tried in military courts and received long prison terms.

The Brotherhood persevered politically, however. It won seventeen seats in the 2000 parliamentary elections despite alleged electoral fraud. In 2005, it took an unprecedented eighty-eight seats in the People's Assembly, the largest number any opposition group had ever won. Almost immediately, the Mubarak regime clamped down on the group by imprisoning the deputy guide and other leaders, sentencing them in military courts, and confiscating Brotherhood businesses. Over the next five years, the regime restricted political space generally. In the December 2010 elections, widely considered the most flawed in modern Egyptian history, the ruling party won more than 90 percent of parliamentary seats. When the extent of electoral fraud became apparent, the Brotherhood withdrew from the poll.

Less than two months later, on January 25, 2011, protests to demand sweeping political change erupted in Cairo. Both the regime and the Brotherhood were taken by surprise. Younger Brothers participated in the initial demonstrations, but as individuals. The movement's leaders waited four days before calling on the faithful to join the protests—and only when the scale of the uprising became apparent.

But in the end, the Brotherhood's numbers, organization, and discipline were critical in defending Tahrir Square and other protest sites from Mubarak's security forces. Eighteen days after the uprising began, Mubarak was forced from power by peaceful civil disobedience.

THE UPRISING

The Muslim Brotherhood established a formal political arm, the Freedom and Justice Party, in June 2011. The party's top three leaders came directly from the group's highest body, the Guidance Bureau. Mohammed Morsy was selected as the party's new chief, Essam el Erian was chosen as vice president, and Mohammed Saad el Katatny became the secretary-general. (Katatny was subsequently elected speaker of parliament and resigned as secretary-general.) All three had previously been elected to parliament and were deeply involved in the Brotherhood's political activities. Morsy is an American-educated engineering professor. Erian is a medical doctor and well-known Brotherhood spokesman. And Katatny is a German-educated microbiology professor. Rafiq Habib, a Christian intellectual, was named as a second vice president.

The platform of the party states that it is committed to equality for all Egyptians; pluralism; social justice; human rights; and the freedoms of expression, belief, and worship. It advocates a "civil state" with an Islamic reference, language the Brotherhood has developed to signal that it does not advocate theocratic government. It is committed to popular sovereignty and to the Sharia as the main source of legislation. The party believes that Egypt needs comprehensive reform to overcome decades of authoritarianism, corruption, and mismanagement.

But the uprising also exposed differences within the Brotherhood. After Mubarak's ouster, the movement faced several internal fissures. Younger members, many of whom participated in the uprising, left the movement to establish the new Egyptian Current Party. They had objected to the undemocratic manner in which Freedom and Justice Party leaders were chosen. They differed with the leadership on the role of religion in politics, its rigidity on other issues, and the specific relationship between the movement and its new party. They also resented the marginalization of younger members within the Brotherhood.

The Brotherhood, for example, expelled Abdel Moneim Aboul Fotouh, a charismatic, liberal, and popular figure, in June 2011 after he announced his intention to run for president. The movement had earlier pledged not to run a presidential candidate to allay fears that it would try to dominate Egyptian politics.

Guaranteeing space in the new political era also forced compromises. During the first year after Mubarak's ouster, the Brotherhood's relations with the ruling Supreme Council of the Armed Forces (SCAF) were cautious, pragmatic, and at times uncritical and supportive. Unlike the Tahrir protesters who demanded the immediate transfer of power to civilian authority, the Brotherhood initially accepted the military's political timeline and transition plan, which it calculated would benefit its own interests.

The Brotherhood did not press the military council to fulfill the uprising's specific democratic aspirations. The Brotherhood was reluctant to criticize SCAF's management of the country or the security forces' use of violence against civilian protesters, which resulted in nearly one hundred deaths and thousands of injuries. It also offered only mild criticism of SCAF's decision to try more than 10,000 civilians in military courts. The Brothers even supported the generals' characterization of protesters as troublemakers.

On the issue of a new constitution, the Brotherhood had long advocated a parliamentary system of government, especially after decades of unrestrained presidential power. But the Brotherhood now began to propose a balanced presidential-parliamentary system, a popular idea among other political groups as well. And it stipulated separation of executive, legislative, and judicial authority. It also objected to a SCAF proposal that would have ensured significant powers for the military and effectively placed the generals above civilian control.

The Muslim Brotherhood is generally a conservative and risk-averse organization. Former Deputy Guide Mohammed Habib reflected, "Revolution is not in the Brotherhood lexicon." But the Brotherhood's role in Egyptian politics changed significantly after the 2011 uprising. From an embattled opposition force, the Brotherhood emerged as the largest elected force in Egypt, and its statements and actions reflect this new reality.

KEY POSITIONS

Democracy

The Brothers have long accepted the basic principles and institutions of democracy, such as a multiparty parliament, the separation of powers, and judicial independence. The group's founder ran for parliament in the 1940s. Since the 1980s, the Brotherhood has consistently participated in legislative and other elections, when permitted, despite significant government repression. But the Brothers are not liberal democrats, and some of their views on women, personal freedoms, and minority rights (including the right to run for president) reflect the limits of their liberalism.

Women's Rights

The Brothers accept many rights for women, including the right to work, get an education, and hold public office. But Egypt is socially conservative on gender, sexuality, and social issues, so the Brothers reflect a widely held patriarchal concept of gender that views women as primarily responsible for the family and home.

The Brother's 2007 draft political party platform drew sharp criticism for stipulating that women and Coptic Christians should not be eligible for the presidency. In the guise of the Freedom and Justice Party, the Brothers now say that the party would not nominate a female presidential candidate but would not advocate prohibiting women or Copts from holding the office.

The Muslim Sisters, the female branch of the movement, has played a visible role in election campaigns and social services, but the Sisters' role is not equal to that of their male counterparts. Women are not members of either the Guidance Bureau or Shura Council, the Brothers' governing bodies. The Brotherhood nominated a single female candidate in the 2000 and 2005 elections. After the Mubarak regime instituted a sixty-four-seat quota system for women, the Brothers fielded more female candidates in the 2010 elections. But the ruling military dropped the quota in 2011. (All of Egypt's political parties historically fielded few women as candidates, a practice that continued in democratic elections in 2011 and 2012.) In 2012, the Freedom and Justice Party had the largest number of women in parliament—four.

Minorities

The Brotherhood and its political party claim to support citizenship rights for all Egyptians, regardless of gender or religion. But Copts and liberals are skeptical that the movement believes in equal political rights for religious minorities. The group's 2007 draft manifesto said that Coptic Christians, who make up 10 percent of Egypt's 85 million people, should not be eligible for the presidency. This position was removed from the 2011 party platform.

The United States and the West

The Brothers support relations between the United States and Egypt based on mutual respect and interest. But the movement decries American support for Israel and Arab authoritarian regimes (such as Mubarak's) as well as U.S. intervention in Afghanistan and Iraq.

The first contacts between the Brothers and U.S. Embassy officials were in the late 1980s, but they ended at the request of the Mubarak regime in the early 1990s. After the 2011–12 election, top U.S. State Department officials flew to Cairo to initiate new contacts with Freedom and Justice Party leaders.

Israel

The Brotherhood's long-standing position was that the Camp David Treaty should be put to a national referendum. Like the majority of Egyptians, the group is intensely critical of Israel and supports Palestinian rights, including the right to resist occupation. The movement also gave birth to Hamas, the Islamist Palestinian movement that won the 2006 Palestinian elections, governs Gaza, and justifies violence against Israeli military and civilian targets.

The Brotherhood's current position on Israel reflects its attempt to maneuver between its long-standing ideology and political realities. After Mubarak was ousted, the Brotherhood said that it would honor Egypt's peace treaty with Israel, but like other Egyptian parties, it suggested that the treaty might have to be modified. The Brothers are unlikely to call for abrogating the agreement while at the same time supporting Hamas and the Palestinians in neighboring Gaza.

THE FUTURE

As the dominant power in parliament, the Brotherhood's challenges are daunting. One of the toughest may be negotiating with SCAF, the military panel that assumed control after pressing Mubarak to resign in 2011. The generals pledged to hand over power after the writing of a new constitution and election of a president by mid-2012.

But Egypt has been ruled by military officers since the 1952 revolution, with the armed forces accumulating a large stake in the economy and virtual veto power over key legislative and foreign policy issues. Whatever happens on paper, the real transition of power may take years. And other political actors have been suspicious that the Muslim Brothers will make a deal with the military in the name of their mutual political interests—and at the expense of Egyptian democracy.

The Freedom and Justice Party will also have to negotiate with other parties, both liberal and Islamist, as well as the revolutionary forces of Tahrir Square—some of whom are skeptical about the Brotherhood's commitment to a truly democratic Egypt. The Islamist parties are also not necessarily natural allies on a range of issues.

Egypt's failing economy will be a particularly urgent issue for the Freedom and Justice Party. Even before the 2011 revolution, Egypt's woes were staggering: high unemployment, perennial budget deficits, crumbling health and educational institutions, and 40 percent of the population living at or close to poverty.

A year later, Egypt was reeling from the costs of political change. After the uprising, tourism, the stock market, and foreign investments all plummeted. Foreign reserves dwindled, and Egypt's credit rating was downgraded. Strikes and labor protests proliferated, while the global economic crisis prevented the world from offering more assistance. Yet public expectations have never been higher, with Egyptians expecting an end to corruption, more jobs, the redistribution of wealth, and more social service benefits— almost none of which the Islamists could quickly provide. How the Freedom and Justice Party and others in parliament tackle these important issues will largely determine the country's future.

Samer Shehata, an assistant professor at Georgetown University, is a former fellow at the Woodrow Wilson International Center for Scholars, the National Endowment for the Humanities–American Research Center in Egypt, and the Carnegie Foundation. He is the author of Shop Floor Culture and Politics in Egypt *(2009) and the editor of the forthcoming* Islamist Politics in the Middle East: Movements and Change *(2012).*

CHAPTER 4

Egypt: The New Puritans

Khalil al Anani

S alafism is a new force in Egyptian electoral politics. The rise of ultra-conservative ideologues has been particularly striking because Salafis had previously renounced participating in politics altogether. In Egypt, the Salafis emerged from the political backwater to win the second largest vote in the 2011–12 elections for parliament. They are now poised to play a pivotal role during Egypt's political transition.

Unlike the Muslim Brotherhood, the Salafis historically have been a loose coalition of groups and individual sheikhs who espoused strict interpretations of Islam and called for implementation of Sharia law. To them, the ideal Islamic society emulates the first three generations after the founding of the faith in the seventh century. They generally hold conservative and often illiberal views on gender relations, minority rights, and personal freedoms.

Yet political Salafism is also a heterogeneous phenomenon encompassing different groups with socioreligious views ranging from the far right to the left. Some sheikhs would like to re-create God's rule on earth. Others more modestly want to implement traditional mores and forms of justice. The sheikhs also differ in terms of the time frame and context for implementing Sharia. Some want to begin moving soon; others are committed to gradually implementing the Sharia, even if it takes decades or centuries. The various sheikhs are often stronger locally than nationally, another contrast to the Brotherhood.

As in other Egyptian movements, the Salafis have a generational divide. The older generation tends to be more puritanical, while the younger generation is more willing to reach beyond its own circle. The sheikhs considered the act of suicide by the Tunisian street vendor, which sparked the Arab uprisings, to be forbidden, or *haram*. The older generation of Salafis also did not support the 2011 uprising, whereas many in the younger generation turned out at Tahrir Square and other protest sites. One group of young Salafis launched the Costa Salafis, named after a popular coffee chain and complete with a page on Facebook.

The Salafis developed a large support base by providing grassroots social services, including welfare, medicines, and food for the needy. Although many Salafis are middle-class professionals, they are also religious populists who play to the lower-class resentment against Egyptian elites. Ironically,

Salafis made inroads in Egyptian society partly because the government tolerated their social activities as a counterweight to the more political Muslim Brotherhood. Salafis are often (although not always, as younger members insist) distinguishable by their untrimmed beards and prayer marks on their foreheads, symbols of the practice of their faith.

In Egypt, the chief Salafi political actor is the Salafi Call, or al Dawa al Salafiyya. Its political arm, the Nour Party, was formed only in mid-2011, after the Egyptian uprising ousted President Hosni Mubarak. But within six months, the Nour Party won 25 percent of the vote in the first free and fair election, or 125 of 498 seats in the lower house of parliament. Together with the Muslim Brotherhood, the Islamists captured about 70 percent of the vote.

THE BEGINNING

Salafism in Egypt originated when university students broke away from the Islamic Group, or al Gamaa al Islamiyya, an umbrella network of Islamist factions that emerged in the 1970s to counter leftists and Nasserists (sometimes with the encouragement of President Anwar Sadat's government). By the mid-1970s, the breakaway factions ranged from radical and violent Islamists to conservative but peaceful groups. The students at Alexandria University created their own movement, the Salafi Call, or al Dawa al Salafiyya, in the late 1970s.

The Salafi Call was created largely because of political and ideological differences with other Islamists, particularly the Muslim Brotherhood, which sought to dominate the Egyptian Islamist scene in the 1970s. The Call's chief founder was Sheikh Mohammed Ismail al Moqadim, a surgeon who received his religious education in Saudi Arabia. He was influenced by Saudi Salafi thinkers such as Sheikh Abdel Aziz bin Baz and Sheikh Mohammed ibn Saleh al Othaimin, who were religious leaders of Wahhabism, Saudi Arabia's own brand of Salafism. Saudi Arabia was created by the merger of Wahhabi clerics and the al Saud family.

In Egypt, the movement's epicenter was Alexandria, where Salafism sought to enhance its presence among university students. Unlike the Muslim Brotherhood, the Salafi Call did not have a formal organizational structure. It relied primarily on preaching—known as the call to Islam, or *dawa*—and student outreach in leaflets, Islamic camps, and lectures in the city's mosques. The major Salafi leaders included Sheikh Yasser Burhami, Sheikh Ahmed Farid, Sayyed Abdel Azim, and Mohamed Abdel Fattah.

In 1986, followers founded the Al Furqan Institute for Preparing Preachers, a school for religious education. Al Furqan became the main venue for the Salafi movement. Through the institute, the movement directed Salafi activities across the country through social, youth, and district committees in the 1980s and 1990s. The movement disseminated the Salafi ideology through a growing religious education network, and it published a monthly magazine, *al Dawa*. In 1994, as the movement's influence grew, the government closed the institute, dissolved its executive council, and banned its monthly magazine.

FROM PIETY TO POLITICS

Yet the Salafi Call eschewed politics. Classical Salafism has a long tradition of quietism. Many Salafis believe that political participation is heresy that corrupts Muslims and therefore should be avoided. Moreover, many traditional Salafi scholars prohibit rebellion or revolution against the ruler even if he is unjust or corrupt, as long as he is a Muslim.

In more practical terms, the movement also shunned Egyptian politics because the government provided no political space for any Islamists to participate. Despite their quietism, many Salafi leaders were arrested during President Hosni Mubarak's last decade in power. The movement even remained silent when one of its members, Sayyed Bilal, was arrested and tortured to death in January 2011, a month before Mubarak was toppled. When popular protests erupted against Mubarak, Sheikh Burhami's faction criticized the protesters and called on Salafis to abstain from participating.

After the revolution, however, Salafi leaders became heavily involved in politics. The movement spawned three new political parties: al Nour (Light), al Asala (Authenticity), and al Fadila (Virtue). The three parties formed a coalition—the Islamic Alliance—to field candidates in Egypt's first fully democratic election in 2011–12.

The ideology of all three parties is uncompromising. They advocate rigid application of the Sharia (Islamic jurisprudence), which they believe entails gender segregation, strict Islamic dress for women, and social restrictions such as outlawing alcohol. Abdel Moneim al Shahat, a controversial senior Nour Party official, outraged Egyptians when he dubbed democracy as "forbidden" (*haram*) and "blasphemy" (*kufr*). He described the works of Egyptian Nobel laureate Naguib Mahfouz as "atheist literature" that promoted "prostitution and drugs." Another hardline Salafi leader urged Egyptians not to vote for liberal, secular, or non-Muslim candidates in the elections.

Salafis are socially conservative partly to preserve Egypt's Islamic identity in the face of Westernization and secularism. As a result, they argued that a new constitution should emphasize the role of Sharia in public and political life as well as in private belief. During the new parliament's inaugural session in January 2012, many Salafi members insisted on adding a religious reference to the official oath; they swore to uphold the constitution as long as it did not contradict the Sharia.

ELECTIONEERING

Since the 2011 uprising, Salafis have sought to inject themselves and their ideas into the center of political debates. They were surprisingly well organized in their first elections despite total political inexperience. They tapped into deeply rooted social networks to encourage support for their candidates. They also built alliances and coalitions with different political forces.

Before the parliamentary elections, the Nour and Asala parties joined the Democratic Alliance, led by the Muslim Brotherhood and including the liberal Wafd Party. But the two Salafi parties withdrew from the alliance on the eve of elections after what they perceived as attempts by the Brotherhood to marginalize Salafi candidates. The two Islamist parties then formed an alliance with the Building and Development Party, the political arm of the Islamic Group (al Gamaa al Islamiyya). (Many leaders of the Islamic Group, which had advocated violence against the regime, were imprisoned in the 1980s and 1990s. By the end of the 1990s, the group had formally renounced violence, and many of its members were released. In 2011, the group fielded candidates for parliament through the Building and Development Party.)

The Salafis did well in elections for several reasons. Islamist ideologies do resonate with pious Egyptians, but the Salafis had also delivered social services to the needy for several decades. Loose-knit but entrenched networks had built up around these services among the lower class and lower-middle class, which suffered under Mubarak's economic reforms. The Salafis achieved sweeping victories in some rural constituencies and on the outskirts of Cairo.

The Salafis' hands-on approach was more effective than that of the social networks, based on the twenty-first-century technology used by liberal and secular activists. "They didn't come to our streets, didn't live in our villages, didn't walk in our hamlets, didn't wear our clothes, didn't eat our bread, didn't drink our polluted water, didn't live in the sewage we live in, and didn't experience the life of misery and hardship of the people," explained Salafi leader Sheikh Shaaban Darwish. In addition, said Nour Party spokesman Mohammed Nour, "Other parties are talking to themselves on Twitter, but we are actually on the streets. We have other things to do than protest in Tahrir."

RIVAL ISLAMISTS

Islamist groups won 70 percent of the seats in Egypt's parliament, but the fiercest battles during the first parliamentary elections were actually between different types of Islamists—not between secular candidates and Islamist candidates. The Salafis and the Muslim Brotherhood will not necessarily work together toward a common Islamist political or social agenda in parliament. And the divergence between the two groups—on a range of issues, including interpretation of the Sharia, gender relations, and views on democracy—represents only a segment of a wider Islamist political spectrum.

The Salafis view the Brotherhood as insufficiently Islamist and too compromising. The Brothers, in turn, view Salafi positions as naïve, overly rigid, insufficiently centrist, and inappropriate in a modern Egyptian context. The Brothers have shown during sporadic participation in past parliaments that their primary focus is on politics and not on religious or cultural issues. After the 2011–12 vote, a Freedom and Justice Party leader said its priorities would be "economic reform and reducing poverty ... not (fighting) bikinis and booze."

As the Salafis began scoring well in the phased elections, Nour Party chief Emad Abdel Ghaffour vowed that the party's new members of parliament would not play second fiddle to the Brotherhood. "We hate being followers," Ghaffour told Reuters. "They always say we take positions according to the Brotherhood but we have our own vision.... There might be a consensus but ... we will remain independent.... They always speak of it with reproach." He warned that the Brotherhood might try to "marginalize" Nour's politicians and portray them as "the troublemaking bloc. The experiences of other parties who have allied with them in the past are bitter."

The Nour Party has demonstrated occasional pragmatism in its political outlook. After the 2011–12 election, its leaders reached out to liberal forces in parliament to counter the strength of the Brotherhood's Freedom and Justice Party. Although Salafis favor Islamic rule, the Nour Party's platform called for establishing a "modern state that respects citizenship and coexistence between all people." The party stressed the separation of legislative, executive, and judicial powers. And it emphasized social justice as well as the people's right to elect their leaders and to hold them accountable.

KEY POSITIONS

Democracy

Until the 2011 uprising, the majority of Salafis rejected democracy as a Western construct that was anathema to Islam. Most Egyptian Salafis also rejected the idea of participation in any formal politics. Salafi leaders criticized the mass protests against the Mubarak regime and argued that opposition to a Muslim ruler contravened Islam. But some Salafis did participate in the protests.

The quantum shift in the willingness of Salafis to participate in formal politics does not mean that most accept the principle of democracy. Some say that democracy is a "tool" or an "instrument" that can be used to implement Sharia. Sheikh Yasser Burhami, a leader in the Salafist Call, explained, "We want democracy, but one constrained by God's laws. Ruling without God's laws is infidelity."

Women's Rights

Most Salafis believe that the most important role for women is in the family, as wives and mothers. Many Salafis object to the idea of women in leadership roles, and some claim that women should minimize their activities in the public sphere. The 2011–12 elections mandated that all political parties include at least one woman on their party-list ticket. The Nour Party's female candidates always appeared at the bottom of the ticket. Their faces never appeared on campaign material, and they were instead depicted by a flower or a party symbol.

Some Salafis also call for the separation of boys and girls in educational institutions after the primary level. Although several prominent Salafi leaders have said that they would not force women to wear the veil or the *niqab*, the full-face veil, some Salafis have suggested imposing restrictions on dress in public.

Minorities

The Nour Party and other Salafi parties hold decidedly illiberal views about religious minorities and personal freedoms. They do not subscribe to the principle of full and equal citizenship for all Egyptians, regardless of religion. Several Salafi leaders have said that they oppose full political rights for non-Muslims.

The Salafis draw a distinction between private and political practice. The Nour Party contends that Sharia ensures Christians the right to practice their beliefs, including the right to handle personal status and family affairs according to Christian traditions. But the party has stated that non-Muslims cannot hold the presidency. On the subject of Coptic Christians, who make up 10 percent of Egypt's population, Sheikh Burhami went further. He specifically said, "Copts do not have the right to run for political office in Egypt."

The Salafis take a tough position on Sufi Muslims, a tolerant mystical form of Islam. Burhami has accused them of heresy and of being supported by the United States. He has been even tougher on the Bahai. Burhami said that he opposes allowing the tiny Egyptian Bahai community to hold religious services in Egypt or to list their religion on national identification cards.

The United States and the West

The views of Salafi parties toward the United States are still not clearly defined, however. Although most Salafis are hostile toward Western civilization generally, the Nour Party claims to advocate relations with foreign states based on respect and peaceful coexistence. But Salafis have demanded the release of Sheikh Omar Abdel Rahman, the blind Egyptian cleric convicted in New York after the 1993 World Trade Center bombing. Many Salafis are outspoken against what they view as U.S. meddling in Egypt's domestic affairs on issues of religious freedom.

Israel

The Nour Party has shown some pragmatism in its position on Israel. Its platform does not specifically address the party's stance on Egypt's peace treaty with the Jewish state, although in an interview with Israeli Army radio, a Nour Party spokesman said that the party would respect Egypt's international commitments and would not abrogate the Camp David Treaty. But like the Brotherhood, the Salafis are sympathetic to Palestinian issues and to Hamas.

THE FUTURE

Egyptian Salafism has evolved from a movement that rejected democracy into a major political force, but it is still immature politically. Public opinion polls indicate that the majority of Egyptians support Sharia as the main source of legislation, which was already enshrined in Article 2 of Egypt's constitution. The more contentious issue will be how strictly that provision is implemented or supervised. The Salafis are likely to have a hard time navigating alliances to achieve the movement's political or economic goals because of concerns among both secular parties and the Brotherhood about the ultraconservative Salafi agenda.

The Salafis' economic strategies are somewhat naïve. One of Nour's proposals is to increase medical tourism so that Egypt is a regional center for health care in both Africa and the Arab world. Given the state of Egyptian health care, that proposal would not be a quick fix for the country's profound economic woes.

Yet despite their conservatism and inexperience, the Salafis have demonstrated their adaptability to Egypt's new political environment and their success in amassing popular support—more so than any secular or liberal party. The Salafis' influence will depend on how Nour and other newly established parties work in parliament—and learn to compromise to win majority support in a democracy.

Khalil al Anani is a scholar of Middle East politics at the School of Government and International Affairs at Durham University in Britain. His books include Elections and Transition in the Middle East in the Post-revolutionary Era *(forthcoming),* Religion and Politics in Egypt After Mubarak *(2011),* Hamas: From Opposition to Power *(2009), and* The Muslim Brotherhood in Egypt: Gerontocracy Fighting against Time *(2008).*

CHAPTER 5

Tunisia: The Best Bet

Christopher Alexander

Tunisia's Islamist experience may hold the best prospects for a democratic transition in the Arab world. From its early roots in the ideas of the Muslim Brotherhood, Ennahda has evolved into an influential exemplar of a moderate, pragmatic Islamism that pledges to support human rights, pluralism, and democracy. It has developed ties to secular organizations that battled authoritarian rule. It is also attuned to the realities of Tunisian society and politics and, compared to movements elsewhere, is less wedded to a strict universal ideology.

The story of Hamadi Jebali reflects the dramatic transformation of the party. Both were basically banished during the twenty-three-year rule of President Zine al Abidine Ben Ali. The party was outlawed. In 1992, the former engineer and journalist was sentenced to sixteen years in prison for membership in an illegal organization and "attempting to change the nature of the state." Jebali spent eleven of those years in solitary confinement before his release in 2006.

Tunisia's uprising—the first in the Arab world—swept Ben Ali from power in a mere thirty days. Virtually overnight, Ennahda returned to politics. When Tunisians went to the polls in October 2011, Ennahda captured 41.5 percent of the vote, the largest in a field of more than sixty parties. The Islamist party won the right to lead the government. It opted to form a coalition with two secular parties.

Tunisia has since made the transition from autocracy to democracy faster than any other Arab country, but it still faces challenges that could stymie or even set back the pace of change. Ennahda's ability to maintain its moderate Islamism will be tested by stubborn economic difficulties, unrealistically high public expectations, emergence of a vocal Salafist trend, and competitive pressures that come with democracy.

THE BEGINNING

Ennahda traces its roots to the late 1960s, a time of intellectual turmoil across the Arab world. The Arab defeat in the 1967 war generated new criticism of secular nationalism. Within Tunisia, a dramatic shift in economic policy prompted many intellectuals to conclude that President Habib Bourguiba's government lacked clear principles.

In this environment, a group of religious thinkers came together in an organization called the Association for the Safeguard of the Koran. The government had established the association to counter its foes on the left. Most of the early Islamists grew up in religious families of modest means and received a religious education. Some Islamists also spent time in Syria and Egypt, where they were exposed to the teachings of the Muslim Brotherhood.

This social and educational background put Tunisia's early Islamists at odds with the culture and values of Tunisia's secular, francophone elite. A young philosophy teacher named Rachid al Ghannouchi emerged as the group's leader. Ghannouchi later reflected, "I remember we used to feel like strangers in our own country. We have been educated as Muslims and as Arabs, while we could see the country totally molded in the French cultural identity."

Tunisia's early Islamists focused primarily on religious and cultural issues. Like their counterparts across the region, they blamed Arab military and social crises on foreign ideologies that pulled Arabs away from their religious and cultural roots. They worked to educate Tunisians about Islamic religious and cultural values through lectures and writing. Trained in language and religion, and mindful of the government's patronage, the movement's leaders paid little attention to politics.

THE 1970S: DEEPER INTO POLITICS

Tunisia's Islamists were pulled deeper into politics in the 1970s by economic discontent and mounting opposition to Bourguiba's authoritarianism. Most of the opposition initially came from leftist student and labor organizations. The Islamists realized that if they wanted to reach a broader audience, they had to talk about more than religion and identity. After a government crackdown on leftist student organizations in 1971–72, Islamists stepped in and began recruiting in secondary school and university campuses. As early as 1973, the government began to fear that it was losing control of the social force it had supported as a counter to the left.

Three developments helped the Islamists develop a stronger political orientation. First, after Anwar Sadat began releasing Muslim Brothers from Egyptian jails, several of them traveled to Tunisia. Their influence gave stronger political content to Tunisian Islamism. Second, in 1978, a bloody crackdown on the country's labor union created a political void that the Islamists again began to fill. And third, the 1979 Iranian Revolution provided an Islamic vocabulary for talking about economic and social issues.

But the Iranian Revolution also increased the Tunisian government's concerns about the Islamists. The regime shut down Islamist publications and accused activists of exploiting Islam for political purposes. To counter these charges, the Islamists emphasized their rejection of violence and Iranian-style theocracy. They also took steps to create a stronger organizational structure. In September 1979, the Islamists established a new organization called the Islamic Group.

THE 1980S: BUILDING A PARTY

In the early 1980s, Bourguiba tried to bolster support by legalizing a handful of opposition parties. Hoping to join the club, the Islamic Group changed its name to the Islamic Tendency Movement (MTI). The party published a platform that rejected violence and advocated human rights, democracy, and political pluralism.

Bourguiba viewed the Islamists as backward fanatics who would destroy the progressive and pro-Western country he was building. He rejected the movement's bid for legal recognition and launched the first of several crackdowns that jailed thousands of Islamists in the mid-1980s. By the summer of 1987, Tunisia teetered on the brink of civil war. The looming prospect of violent chaos prompted Prime Minister Zine al Abidine Ben Ali to depose Bourguiba in November 1987.

The repression of the 1980s opened important fissures within the Islamist movement. To the left of the mainstream, progressive Islamists argued that Ghannouchi should develop a more sophisticated Islamism that reflected the specific characteristics of Tunisian society. On the right, a more militant and doctrinaire trend rejected democratic politics and argued that rebellion was the only way to topple Bourguiba.

The repression also helped the Islamic Tendency Movement forge ties with the human rights league, the labor movement, and other opposition parties. Regardless of the philosophical differences between them, all of these groups shared a common desire to replace Bourguiba with a democratic system that respected human and political rights. Increasingly, the MTI cast its struggle in these terms. In turn, other organizations rallied to the movement's defense as Bourguiba's repression intensified.

1987–91: BEN ALI'S BRIEF HONEYMOON

Ben Ali began his tenure with a wave of reforms that released political prisoners and relaxed some controls on political life. MTI leaders praised the new president for removing Bourguiba and saving the country from chaos. In another bid for legal recognition, they changed the party's name to the Ennahda (Renaissance) Party in order to comply with a new law that forbade party names to contain religious references.

Ben Ali, however, did not legalize Ennahda. But he also did not want to provoke a party that enjoyed strong popular support and a clandestine organization. When Tunisians went to the polls in 1989, the government did not allow Ennahda to run lists as a legal party, but it did allow Islamist candidates to run as independents.

The Islamists' clear victory over secular opposition parties ended Ben Ali's honeymoon with Ennahda. Between 1989 and 1992, arbitrary arrests, passport seizures, and incidents of torture steadily increased.

Unable to organize or preach within the country, Ghannouchi fled Tunisia one month after the 1989 elections. More militant Islamists within Ennahda and other organizations built protest networks on university campuses and in underprivileged neighborhoods. As marches and demonstrations increased, so did the police crackdown.

In February 1991, three Islamist activists burned a ruling party office in the Bab Souika quarter of Tunis. This incident—which Ennahda condemned—along with the government's claim to have uncovered a broader revolutionary plot, provided the regime with an excuse to launch a full assault.

1992–2000: THE DARKEST CHAPTER

Throughout the 1990s, the Tunisian government steadily intensified its campaign against Ennahda. From his base in London, Ghannouchi maintained contact with supporters in Europe and the Arab world. He also was able to communicate with key activists in Tunisia. However, Ben Ali's repression destroyed much of Ennahda's organization and forced the remnants deep underground.

Ennahda did not cease to exist. Because security forces often harassed the families of political prisoners, Ben Ali's crackdown created serious economic difficulties for thousands of Tunisians who never went to jail. During this period, Ennahda maintained a sparse clandestine network of activists, who channeled financial resources and other forms of assistance to prisoners' families. The party also benefited from the support of human rights activists and some secular politicians who defended Ennahda as part of their broader effort to build a coalition against Ben Ali.

2000–11: REBUILDING

Tunisia's political environment began to change in the early years of the new century. Economic stagnation, rising unemployment, and mounting evidence of grotesque corruption within Ben Ali's family generated frustration that spread deeper and wider than in the 1990s. Even members of the ruling party began to feel the grasping hands of Ben Ali's kleptocratic family. Ben Ali also faced stronger international pressure on human rights, prompting the president to allow a bit more space for opposition activity.

Ennahda activists, many of whom had been in jail since the 1980s and 1990s, began to rebuild the party's organization. By 2005, Ennahda and several other opposition groups agreed to a joint platform of demands. In the deal, Ennahda committed itself to a multiparty democracy and to the progressive rights that Tunisian women by then enjoyed.

As an organization, Ennahda did not play an important role in the December 2010 rebellion that drove Ben Ali from power. In the months that followed, however, its organization and financial resources made it the most effective party in Tunisia. Ennahda enjoyed name recognition, national grassroots structures, money, and credibility that no other party could equal. It rallied a broad base that stretched beyond religious voters to include social conservatives, human rights activists, and voters who saw Ennahda as a representative of Tunisian identity.

KEY POSITIONS

Islam and Democracy

Ennahda has repeatedly pledged its commitment to competitive multiparty politics. Since Ben Ali's fall, the party has placed particular emphasis on creating a parliamentary system that prevents the concentration of power in one person's hands.

Many secular Tunisians and outsiders question the sincerity of Ennahda's commitment to democracy. Time will tell, but a strong case can be made that democracy serves Ennahda's interests. Over the long term, Ennahda leaders suggest that numbers are on their side. They believe that most Tunisians hold views that are closer to Ennahda's than to the views of Tunisia's secular parties. If the leaders are correct, then a system that relies on the expressed will of the people will generate good results for Ennahda.

In the short term, however, Ennahda cannot govern alone. Its leaders realize that they benefited in the October 2011 elections from name recognition and from broad sympathy for Ennahda because the party bore the brunt of Ben Ali's repression. These advantages will not last long. Once the Constituent Assembly completes the new constitution, Tunisians will go back to the polls to elect a new National Assembly. From now on, voters will evaluate Ennahda on the basis of its record in government, not in opposition. To generate economic growth and jobs, Ennahda needs the cooperation of social and economic actors who do not share its social and religious views.

Ennahda also needs the cooperation of other political parties. Ennahda received 41.5 percent of the vote in an election that attracted barely more than 50 percent of eligible voters. In other words, although Ennahda received more votes than any other party, well under 50 percent of the adult population actually voted for Ennahda. If it is true that a majority of Tunisians are more conservative than the secular parties, it is not necessarily true that this majority will vote for Ennahda. Unless and until that becomes true, Ennahda needs coalition partners to build a majority that can pass legislation in the National Assembly.

If Ennahda cannot govern alone, it also does not want to govern alone—at least not now. As Ghannouchi said during a November 2011 visit to Washington, D.C., "The next phase [of Tunisia's transition] is a sensitive phase. There are big challenges. It is an adventure for a single party to go it alone during this phase." Tunisia faces serious social and economic challenges that Ennahda cannot solve before Tunisians go to the polls again in 2013. Ennahda wants to share power because it wants to share responsibility for failing to meet popular expectations.

Ennahda insists that it does not seek to impose Sharia. In 2011, it resisted efforts by more extreme Islamists to rewrite the constitution to make it more Islamic. In assembling the government that will rule until the next elections, Ennahda also allowed competent secular technocrats to fill important ministries.

The combination of words and deeds suggested that Ennahda does not see Islam as a set of universal obligations or as a guide to policymaking. Instead, it sees Islam as a source of cultural identity and personal belief as well as the source of Ennahda's commitment to ethical government. Because Ennahda believes that most Tunisians already are more religious than either previous governments or secular parties, the party does not need to wage a campaign to make Tunisian society more Islamic. It simply wants to remove restrictions that prevent Muslims from practicing their faith as they choose.

Other Religions

Ennahda has stated clearly that it supports the rights of Jews and Christians to practice their faiths in Tunisia. On one hand, it is an easy commitment to make since Tunisia's population is 99 percent Sunni Muslim. Ennahda does not have to contend with the sectarian tensions that complicate politics in Egypt or Syria.

On the other hand, the emergence of a vocal Salafist trend gives real significance to Ennahda's position. When Ismail Haniyeh, the Hamas prime minister of the Gaza government, arrived in Tunis in January 2012, a handful of Salafists greeted him at the airport with cries of "Crush the Jews" and "Kill the Jews." Four days later, Ennahda issued a statement that condemned those slogans and reaffirmed the equal rights of Tunisia's Jewish citizens.

Ennahda's commitment to religious freedom, which Ghannouchi has explained at length, appears sincere. More pragmatically, this commitment costs Ennahda little and could generate important benefits. The new government realizes that Tunisian Jewish communities in Europe, North America, and Israel could make important contributions to the country's economic recovery. President Moncef Marzouki, elected by the Constituent Assembly in December 2011, recently called on Jews of Tunisian origin to return home and help rebuild the country.

The United States

Cordial relations with the United States date to the early days of the American republic. Washington supported Tunisia's struggle for independence, and Tunisia's foreign policy generally has supported U.S. interests in the region even when those positions generated criticism in the Arab world.

On several occasions, Ennahda leaders have harshly criticized the United States, particularly in the early 1990s. The movement felt that Washington supported Ben Ali's dictatorship out of an unrealistic fear of Islamist violence. In 2012, Ennahda leaders contend that Americans should see those criticisms in context. They reflect Ennahda's need to rally its base in the face of deepening repression. Referring to how his position has changed since that time, Ghannouchi said in a recent speech, "Only stones don't change in twenty years; people do."

Ennahda may not like aspects of U.S. policy in other parts of the Arab world, particularly Palestine. But it does not see those issues as central to Tunisia's welfare. As Ghannouchi's 2011 trip to Washington illustrated, what matters now is maintaining American support of Tunisia's democratic transition and receiving development assistance. Ennahda is not prepared to allow differences of opinion on tangential issues to disrupt the relationship.

Women's Issues

No single constituency has expressed greater concern about Ennahda's rise than Tunisian women. Tunisia was long known for its progressive legal framework on women's rights. The 1956 Personal Status Code provided the foundation for this framework.

Ennahda has said repeatedly that it will respect the Personal Status Code and all other rights women enjoyed under Ben Ali. The party has claimed it wants to expand opportunities for women by eliminating workplace harassment and other inequities. When conflict broke out in December 2011 between Salafists and secularists over the right to wear the veil in universities, Ennahda called on university officials to resolve the conflict "without infringing in any shape or form on a woman's fundamental right to choose her own clothing.... We live within the dynamics of a fledgling democracy, and we must respect democratic principles."

Women have long played an active role within Ennahda. Women sustained much of the family support network during the darkest days of Ben Ali's repression. Ennahda was one of the first parties to support the new rule requiring political parties to include equal numbers of men and women on their candidate lists.

Israel-Palestine

Ennahda clearly supports Palestinian aspirations. But it sees the struggle as a Palestinian affair. Israel and Palestine are thousands of miles away. European and North African neighbors are closer and much more important. Jews of Tunisian origin can be important allies in the country's development effort. In mid-2011, Ennahda opposed an effort by some parties to craft an agreement that would have required the new constitution to forbid normalized relations with Israel.

OTHER ISLAMISTS

Tunisia's Islamist movement has never been a monolith. Ennahda itself is a diverse party. Since the early 1980s, more extreme organizations have criticized the mainstream's decision to work through democratic political institutions.

Since Ben Ali's fall, a Salafist trend has become much more active in Tunisia. Recent estimates put the number of Salafist supporters at 2,000 to 3,000. The trend contains a number of organizations, but two are the most visible in 2012: Hizb al Tahrir, which splintered from the Muslim Brotherhood, has existed in Tunisia since the early 1980s. Ansar al Sharia was established in April 2011.

The Salafist trend rallies around a handful of positions:

- A rejection of democratic politics
- A demand for an Islamic state with the Koran and Sharia as the basis for the constitution
- An elimination of political parties and elections as infringements on God's sovereignty
- Gender segregation and public prayer on university campuses
- A return to the veil in universities and public offices

The Salafist trend is active in several working-class neighborhoods in and around Tunis, and it also reaches into the regions of the country that felt the strongest effects of the revolt last winter. The movement controls a network of mosques and enjoys financial support from outside the country.

Despite their small numbers, the Salafists have made a dramatic mark on the early days of Tunisia's new government. As noted earlier, they have been particularly active on university campuses. They have demonstrated outside the National Assembly. They also have attacked cinemas, bars, and houses of prostitution.

THE FUTURE

In 2011, Tunisians carried out a comparatively smooth transition, which included passing a sequence of reforms and holding the first free elections. Several factors were key: the military was willing to stay out of politics, Islamists and secular leaders worked together, and voters elected candidates willing to work across ideological lines. Those factors have made Tunisia a model for the region. Nevertheless, Tunisia's fledgling democracy and the mainstream Islamist movement face daunting challenges.

Managing the Economy and Popular Expectations

Frustration over unemployment and regional economic disparities helped to spark the rebellion against Ben Ali. By the first anniversary of the uprising in 2012, the rate of unemployment still hovered around 15 percent nationally; it was higher in interior regions. The more prosperous coastal areas still felt like a different country from the interior. The economy registered negative growth in 2011, and Western assistance has been slow to arrive.

Tunisia enjoys a prime geographic location and an educated population. But the country has few natural resources, and many of its traditional exports struggle in deeply competitive markets. Identifying sectors that can generate growth, attract investors, boost tourism, expand exports, and distribute growth and jobs more equitably will take time. Achieving these goals will also force the government to make hard choices between policies that attract investment and create jobs for the long term and policies that increase incomes short term.

Many Tunisians understand these challenges. Yet hardship also breeds impatience. In the first year after the uprising, hundreds of sit-ins and strikes crippled the economy. The new government pleaded with the population—to little avail—to stop the protests, which were making it even more difficult to jumpstart a recovery.

Public impatience creates a particular challenge for Ennahda. Failure to address popular grievances could make Ennahda vulnerable to criticism when election season begins again in 2013. To protect itself from the left, Ennahda could be tempted to fall back on grandiose, but irresponsible, populism. To protect itself from the right, Ennahda could take a more conservative stand on cultural issues. Perhaps most dangerous, Ennahda could become less tolerant of criticism and use its new powers to craft political rules that handicap political opposition.

Managing the Salafists

The Salafists' confrontational rhetoric and tactics have put Ennahda in a difficult position. Ennahda leaders hope that a more open political environment will moderate the Salafists' views. When pressed, they have also publicly denounced Salafist positions on the constitution, women's issues, and the use of anti-Semitic rhetoric. These statements, however, have not always been timely, which has led critics to argue that Ennahda may not truly reject the Salafists' message.

Salafists are only a small fraction of the Islamist trend, but criticizing their positions risks alienating conservative members of Ennahda's base and acknowledging the Salafists as important political players. But failure to repudiate the Salafists' more extreme rhetoric would reinforce doubts about Ennahda's ultimate intentions.

New Political Institutions

Decades of dictatorship have given many Tunisians a strong allergy to executive power. Ennahda supports a parliamentary system that vests substantial power in a prime minister who is more directly accountable to voters than a president.

But making power accountable also carries risks, especially in a country that faces serious social and economic challenges. Meeting these challenges will require a state that can make difficult choices and execute them efficiently. As the constituent assembly rewrites the constitution, Ennahda will need to create a firewall against authoritarian relapse without depriving the country of decisive leadership.

Ennahda also must support institutions that clearly divide power and that can sustain changes in personnel at the top. The current government is led by three men—President Marzouki, Prime Minister Hamadi Jebali, and Moustafa Ben Jaafar, the president of the Constituent Assembly—with long histories as partners struggling against authoritarian rule. Their history of trust has aided the new government. But the arrangement between the president, the prime minister, and the speaker of the Constituent Assembly did not resolve questions about the division of powers among them. A key challenge will be clarifying the division of powers in ways that do not rely on shared histories or views.

As the major power in government, the Islamist movement is tasked with constructing institutions to protect minority rights for women, Jews, Christians, and others—a question that vexes Tunisia's secularists. Absent institutions that guarantee protections, creeping social conservatism and political competition could push Ennahda to the right—and to violations of minority rights that are justified not with the language of Sharia, but with the language of majority rule.

Christopher Alexander is the John and Ruth McGee director of the Dean Rusk International Studies Program at Davidson College. In addition to several articles on politics in North Africa, he is the author of Tunisia: Stability and Reform in the Modern Maghreb (2010).

CHAPTER 6

Libya: Rebuilding from Scratch

Manal Omar

Libya's Islamists quickly rose from the ashes after the 2011 uprising that ousted Colonel Moammar Qaddafi. They had been pushed into exile or the underground during his forty-two-year rule. Libyans, who are culturally conservative even if they do not actively practice the faith, responded enthusiastically to Islamic political parties as they struggled to rebuild a new order.

One year later, the new Islamists were deep into developing progressive theory, but they were still seriously devoid of political experience. They were also plagued by layers of contradictions between their traditional past and the modern political organizations they were trying to create. As a result, Libya's Islamists faced a sort of existential crisis. Carving out sufficient political space often meant promoting themselves from a nationalist platform or attaching themselves to tribal or regional groups that undercut their own broader Islamic agenda.

The Islamic movement in Libya has been strongly influenced by the Sufi tradition of the Sanussi Order, an unusual and even unlikely blend of Islamic mysticism and strident Salafism. Until 2011, Islamist ideas were shaped primarily in exile. Libyans even attribute the survival of the Islamists to their experiences in the West, where many came into contact with the ideas of the Muslim Brotherhood while students in the United States and Europe. Islamist ideas were banned in Libya, where Qaddafi once compared the movement to a cancer. But they were freely accessed in the West.

Islamist ideas in post-Qaddafi Libya are deeply nuanced. The country's social conservatism makes any perceived criticism of Islam political suicide. Yet in another seeming contradiction, the same conservatism makes most Libyans reject the notion of Islam as the primary or only platform for a political party. Islamic principles are instead a given. The issue is how Islamic values will shape policy to set the oil-rich North African country back on track. Libyans have also been vocal nationwide about fighting the emergence of Islamic extremism. The framework of Islamic political parties that emerged since the revolution reflects an awareness of all three preferences.

As of 2012, Libya had two large Islamic political parties: The older Libyan Islamic Group is a local branch of the Muslim Brotherhood founded in Egypt. The new Libyan Islamic Movement for Change is a reincarnation of the Libyan Islamic Fighting Group, a jihadist movement that renounced violence in 2006.

THE BEGINNING

Islam has been central to modern Libyan political life for a century. It was introduced by the Sanussi Order, founded in Mecca in 1837 by Mohammed ibn Ali as Sanussi. The Algerian-born cleric sought to regenerate Muslim identity and spirituality. While living in Mecca, he crafted a new order that was austere but rejected fanaticism. The so-called Sanussiyya movement was revivalist, bringing together the Sufi Islamic tradition and religious reforms that looked to the life of the Prophet Mohammed as a social model, which was also the original concept of Saudi Arabia's Wahhabism. Sanussi moved his new order to Libya in the mid-nineteenth century.

After the Italian occupation of Libya in 1911, the largest anticolonial campaign—a form of jihad—was led by the Sanussi Order. The resistance was symbolized by Omar al Mukhtar, a religious leader and instructor educated by the Sanussi brotherhood. In 1951, when Libya gained independence from Italy, Mohammed Idris, a grandson of Sanussi, was crowned king. His legitimacy as a leader stemmed from the religious order, which he then headed. As King Idris I, he ruled until his ouster in a military coup led by Qaddafi in 1969.

The Sanussi Order thrived in the equally austere Bedouin tribal culture of eastern Libya, or Cyrenaica, which is also where the rebellion against Qaddafi was later launched. Qaddafi clearly viewed the revival of the order as a threat. During Qaddafi's rule, Mukhtar's grave was moved from Benghazi to a remote area beyond Tobruk in an attempt to minimize both Mukhtar's place and Sanussi influence in Libyan history. After Qaddafi was toppled, Mukhtar was revived as the symbol of resistance—eighty years after his death in 1931. Posters, key chains, and graffiti bearing Mukhtar's image became visible or available for sale across Benghazi.

The Libyan branch of the Muslim Brotherhood emerged in the 1950s, when King Idris offered refuge to Egyptian members fleeing the rule of Gamal Abdel Nasser. Many Egyptians offered political asylum in Libya taught at Libyan universities, where they built a strong student following. Over time, the students created their own branch of the Brotherhood.

DICTATORSHIP AND DOCTRINES

Like leaders of many authoritarian regimes, Qaddafi used religion to try to gain wider legitimacy. He called for imposition of Sharia law and banned alcohol, nightclubs, and prostitution. He also pushed Arab nationalism and socialism as cornerstones of nation building. But Qaddafi was the only secular leader to introduce doctrinal changes and innovations to Islam.

The former military officer often went on national television to challenge traditional religious scholars. In a controversial statement, he once claimed that the Koran was the only source of authority for establishing Islamic law—a contention that marginalized the Hadith (the sayings of the Prophet Mohammed) as well as religious authorities such as the *ulema* (Islamic scholars) and the *fuqaha* (jurists). Qaddafi then began making his own interpretations based on his reading of the Koran.

To eliminate potential opposition, Qaddafi disbanded the Muslim Brotherhood when he came to power. In the 1970s, the Brotherhood existed largely in exile. It was not able to reestablish a presence inside Libya until the late 1980s. It operated predominately underground, although it was able to establish its own *shura* (consultative) council inside the country. Ironically, the Brotherhood was sustained partly by the Qaddafi regime's policy of sending students on scholarships overseas, where young Libyans were reintroduced to the Brotherhood's philosophy.

As in other Brotherhood branches elsewhere in the region, Libya's members came largely from the middle class and professional class. They were not all like minded, however. In an important split, one faction viewed the Brotherhood as a pan-Islamic movement and eagerly sought coordination with Cairo. Other factions argued that the movement should adapt the Brotherhood's general principles to the specific Libyan national context.

During the 1970s and 1980s, the first jihadist cells were also created in Libya. They gathered around radical sheikhs who advocated armed struggle. In the 1980s, young militants mobilized around the call for jihad in Afghanistan against the Soviet Union. After the Soviet Union's withdrawal from Afghanistan in 1989, most militants returned to Libya and shifted their focus to the injustices of the Qaddafi regime.

RECONCILIATION

For most of his four-decade rule, the Qaddafi regime justified cracking down on Islamic political groups in the name of state security and counterterrorism. But in 2006, Saif al Islam, Qaddafi's son and political adviser, began negotiating reconciliation with the Islamists.

Saif al Islam pushed for rehabilitation of imprisoned Islamists in exchange for recognition of the government, renunciation of violence, and formal revisions of the Islamists' doctrines. The reforms played out in phases. More than one hundred members of the Muslim Brotherhood were released in 2006, and by 2008, hundreds of members of the Libyan Islamic Fighting Group had also been freed.

Among the key authors of the 2006 reconciliation agreement was Abdelhakim Belhaj (then a member of the Libyan Islamic Fighting Group), who secured his release from prison through the agreement. He represented the evolution of Libya's jihadis in many ways. He had gone to Afghanistan in 1988, where he fought the Soviets, and remained until 1992. In 2004, he was detained in Malaysia and brought to Thailand, where U.S. Central Intelligence Agency questioned him. He was eventually handed over to Libyan authorities, who placed him in prison.

The reconciliation document he helped craft marked a pivotal turning point in Libya's Islamist history. It redefined the rules of engagement for jihadists and repudiated the al Qaeda doctrine that justified killing civilians. The deal explicitly stated that Islamic tradition forbids the targeting of women, children, elderly people, religious leaders, traders, and unarmed civilians.

AFTER THE REVOLUTION

After Qaddafi's ouster, Libya's Islamist politics solidified around two formal organizations—the Libyan Islamic Movement for Change and the Libyan Islamic Group, which is the Brotherhood offshoot—and several smaller "gatherings" around prominent Islamic figures such as Sheikh Ali Sallabi and Sheikh al Sadiq al Gharyani. There are also informal armed Islamic groups, particularly in the eastern provinces such as Derna. But these groups have not been transformed into major political players.

Outside of tribal and regional ties, Libya's most recognized sociopolitical organization is the Libyan Islamic Group. It claims to have participated in the revolution from the onset by providing food, aiding the wounded, and conducting humanitarian missions. It soon vowed to create a moderate political party. It organized events where women were invited to attend and speak. It sponsored new civil society organizations. Less than a year after Qaddafi's ouster, the Libyan Islamic Group's membership had doubled.

The Muslim Brotherhood offshoot enjoyed three advantages. First, it was able to work directly with the people—and gain popularity on the streets—through humanitarian and economic programs. These social contracts gave it a strong advantage over other political parties.

Second, the Libyan Islamic Group was part of an international pan-Islamic movement able to share lessons for grassroots mobilization and political participation. More than other Libyan groups, it demonstrated political maturity by ensuring that its members voted as a bloc, rather than as individuals, in new government organizations. This was particularly true in local councils.

Finally, the Libyan Islamic Group demonstrated transparency. In November 2011, it held a four-day national conference to elect leaders. No other political party had held a national conference, and leadership negotiations had often taken place behind closed doors. During the national conference, the plenary assembly elected Bashir Kabti as the Muslim Brotherhood's general representative.

Kabti was a somewhat controversial choice. He had strong ties to the old regime and was not connected to the original Libyan branch of the Brotherhood. He lacked charisma. And critics charged that he lacked a longer-term national vision, a drawback that could diminish support. Some felt he had stronger loyalty to the Brotherhood's pan-Islamic movement than to the focused mission of transforming Libya.

Although its membership has steadily grown, the Libyan Islamic Group may still not be able to win elections on its own, a weakness that has characterized trends in other Arab countries since 2011. It has done well at the social grassroots level—specifically among the lower socioeconomic classes—in terms of mobilization, education, community programs, and youth programs. But some Libyans remain suspicious of the movement's long-term goals, so the Brotherhood offshoot may also need to enter into broad coalitions and alliances to rule the country.

The second largest Islamist party is the Libyan Islamic Movement for Change, the reincarnation of the militant Libyan Islamic Fighting Group. The party was cofounded by Belhaj, the head of the Tripoli Military Council, in August 2011.

Belhaj has also been a leader in holding the National Transitional Council accountable, a position that has earned him popularity. His main grievance is that the council's agenda is too secular and too focused on the West's goals for Libya—issues that have generally caused significant tension between Islamists and the Western-oriented members of the transition government.

Belhaj and Sallabi have both warned of "extremist secularism"—a message that strongly resonates in Libya. In September 2011, Belhaj explained this view in an op-ed piece in *The Guardian*:

> What worries us is the attempt of some secular elements to
> isolate and exclude others. Libya's Islamists have announced
> their commitment to democracy; despite this, some reject
> their participation and call for them to be marginalised. It
> is as though they want to push Islamists towards a non-
> democratic option by alienating and marginalising them.

Belhaj is well respected for his years in Abu Slim prison, but many Libyans were surprised by his appointment to head the Tripoli Military Council shortly after Qaddafi's ouster. Rebels reported that Belhaj was not present during the fall of Qaddafi's compound and arrived only shortly afterward, in time to deliver the victory speech. Belhaj has also faced accusations that Qatari funding was funneled directly to him, triggering concern within the transition government that his party has an unfair advantage over other parties.

The political direction of the "gatherings"—whether they will join one of the two formal parties or emerge as independent political entities—was still uncertain in early 2012. The individual clerics had not expressed loyalty to any party. In Tripoli, Sheikh Gharyani was widely credited with taking the revolution from its roots in the east to the capital of Tripoli in the west with his address to the nation in August 2011.

Under Qaddafi, Gharyani had been a former head of the Supreme Council for Fatwas and a faculty member at Al Fateh University's Department of Islamic Studies. But his political independence was firmly accepted in Libyan society. Sheikh Sallabi, widely viewed as the most influential Islamist leader in Libya, spent many years in prison under Qaddafi. Sallabi is often linked with the Muslim Brotherhood.

KEY POSITIONS

There is no monolithic voice that speaks for the Islamists in Libya. The two main political parties have not issued detailed platforms; their positions are discerned largely from the speeches or behavior of their individual leaders. The two groups vary on some issues; they also have internal divisions. Both are, in effect, still learning.

Democracy

Both parties have taken initial steps that reflect interest in nonviolent participatory political action. The Libyan Islamic Group is the only group in Libya to hold a national conference open to all Libyans where the representation was elected.

The Libyan Islamic Movement for Change—which grew out of local jihad cells in the late 1970s and 1980s—has responded to public demands to avoid extremism. Its members agreed in March 2011 to come under full command of the National Transitional Council, thus indicating a willingness to work under a central authority and with other parties—abandoning the guerrilla tactics that had been the trademark of the Libyan Islamic Movement for Change's predecessor, the Libyan Islamic Fighting Group, in the 1990s.

Islam

The core dispute is not over whether Islam will play a role in the new Libya but over what specific role it will play. The greatest concern is coming from within the Islamist movement. Some members are concerned about a new brand of Islam intolerant to other interpretations, such as the rich historical Sufi tradition. Some Islamists even fear a new breed of extremism. Other Libyans fear a clash of Islamic ideologies. Islamists often tend to lose their Islamic identity once they reach power and turn into political entities.

Therefore, many Libyans express a fear of political Islam while simultaneously calling for a central role for the faith within the new state. What may seem to be a contradiction is extremely clear in the Libyan mindset.

Secularism

Libyans are overwhelmingly conservative and call for Islam to have a large role in the nation-building process, but the sparsely populated North African country also has a strong secularist movement. For four decades, Qaddafi fostered a fear of Islamists. In a 1989 speech, for example, he said that Islamists were "more dangerous than AIDS."

Women

Libyan women have generally not fared well under either secularists or Islamists. In January 2012, the National Transitional Council dropped a proposal to create a 10 percent minimum quota for women in parliament. Some Libyan women fear that Islamist parties will further marginalize women—a fear based on what has happened to their counterparts in Iraq, where a drastic decline in elected women is widely attributed to the rise of religious political parties. But female activists scoff at the prospect of living in a Taliban-like nation, even as many reject the Western idea of women's liberation.

Minorities

In terms of minorities, many Islamists point out that historically the oppression of minorities in Libya has been the result of a clash between the Arab cultures and was not tied to Islamic principles. For example, the Berbers do not have any problem with Islam and are more likely to clash with the notion of Libya as an Arab state than with the notion of Libya as an Islamic state. The focus among the minorities within Libya is on fighting for their cultural rights, and Islamists argue that this objective does not contradict any Islamic principles. Minorities would be able to speak their local language, have their own schools, and name their children as they chose.

The United States and the West

All political parties have expressed gratitude to the United States and to the North Atlantic Treaty Organization forces for support in overthrowing Qaddafi. There is generally a keen interest in maintaining positive relationships with Western nations while also trying to secure sovereignty during the transition process. Many of the Brotherhood members were educated in the West, which may foster a basis for international contacts.

Israel

Like many Arab autocrats, Qaddafi used the Palestinian cause to focus on an external enemy and promote himself as a regional hero. He even instituted a special mandatory tax to support jihad in Palestine. But since his ouster, there has been an unspoken consensus across politics that the Arab-Israeli conflict is simply not a priority for Libya during the transition. Israel is also not a neighbor, so the conflict is literally not an urgent frontline issue.

Overall, all Libyan parties are still committed to supporting the Palestinian right of self-determination. But the Libyan trend is to remain in the background and delegate responsibility to the Palestinians themselves.

THE FUTURE

For the foreseeable future, the status of Islam as a religion and of Islamists as political forces will play a dynamic role in the nation-building process in Libya. The centrality of Islam has been officially recognized by the National Transitional Council's leader. Council chairman Mustafa Abdul Jalil gave two public addresses highlighting the importance of Islam. The first was after the fall of Tripoli in September 2011, and the second was in October 2011, when he announced the liberation of the country.

Yet Libyans across generations and religious affiliations emphasize the central purpose of the revolution as freedom, justice, and opportunities. Many say they are ready to protect these principles with their lives and see the framework—secular or Islamic—as secondary. Libyans also appear widely intent on eradicating all forms of extremism.

Libya has several advantages over other Arab countries in transition. First, more than 90 percent of Libyans are Sunni Muslims who follow the Maliki school of thought. Maliki is the more moderate of the four traditional schools of jurisprudence. Libya's Islamic movements are also partly rooted in a Sufi tradition, notably the Sanussi Order. The country also has vast oil wealth but a small population of some 6.5 million, factors that could help prevent the kinds of economic tensions that are troubling other Arab countries.

Manal Omar is the director of the North Africa, Iraq, and Iran programs for the United States Institute of Peace. She was a member of the Libya Stabilization Team under the National Transitional Council formed during the revolution. She was previously a regional program manager for Oxfam GB and led humanitarian responses for Yemen, Lebanon, the Palestinian Territories, and Iraq. Omar is the author of Barefoot in Baghdad *(2010).*

CHAPTER 7

Algeria: Bloody Past and Fractious Factions

David B. Ottaway

Riding the regional political wave, Algeria's leading Islamic party proclaimed on New Year's Day 2012 that it intended to become the primary political force in the Arab world's second most populous country. But unlike in Egypt and Tunisia, the declaration in Algeria did not mark the first attempt by Islamist politicians to take power. Algeria has had the longest—and darkest—experience with Islamist politics, dating back a generation. As a result, the North African country is far more anxious about what might happen if Islamist parties try again.

Algeria's Islamists arrived at the cusp of power in 1992, when the Islamic Salvation Front was on the verge of winning a parliamentary election in a field of more than fifty parties. On the eve of a runoff vote, however, the Algerian military led a coup against the long-standing president, aborted the election, and arrested Islamist political leaders. With nonviolent Islamist leaders imprisoned, the coup soon spawned an extremist insurgency and a tough military counterinsurgency that plunged the country into civil war for the rest of the decade. More than 100,000 people died in the process.

So, still scarred by the so-called Black Decade, Algeria did not witness a popular pro-democracy uprising in 2011, as happened in Tunisia and Egypt. Yet in some ways, Algeria is way ahead of other Arab countries, where Islamic parties only recently won political office for the first time.

To co-opt Islamist sentiment, Algeria's military appointed members of the Movement of Society for Peace (MSP), a moderate offshoot of Egypt's Muslim Brotherhood, to cabinet jobs in 1995. The movement has held as many as seven ministries ever since. In 2004, it even became part of an alliance with two secular parties that has kept the military-backed president, Abdelaziz Bouteflika, in power since 1999.

Although Algeria's more moderate Islamists have now had a share in the country's governance for seventeen years, their failure to affect the military government's policies has reduced the Islamists' popularity considerably. Algerian Islamists have thus already experienced both the temptations and the pitfalls of serving in governments they do not control. The movement has been criticized for a meager record of accomplishments. In 2009, an MSP faction broke away after charging that the party had nothing to show for fourteen years in government.

Political Islam in Algeria has its own special history. Unlike Islamists elsewhere in North Africa, Algeria's Islamists have been deeply fragmented. Some belong to mystical indigenous Sufi orders. Others cleave either to Saudi Arabia's strict Wahhabism, which is one brand of Salafism, or to Egypt's Muslim Brotherhood. Several hundred Algerian Islamists have followed al Qaeda's call to violent jihad. But the various branches lack dynamic leadership. No towering Islamic figure, such as Tunisia's Sheikh Rachid al Ghannouchi, has emerged to unite Algerian Islamists in their quest for power.

The Algerian military, which has dominated power since 1965, has also masterfully manipulated the myriad Islamic parties and politicians. And even moderate Islamists have been tainted by the blood-drenched insurgency of their extremist brethren. In 2012, a generation later, diehard Islamist remnants remained in several remote outposts.

THE BEGINNING

Algerian Islamists have struggled to revive their cause since French colonial rule systematically suppressed Islam, education in Arabic, and the mere notion of an Algerian identity. Algeria was declared part of France and French culture forever. French arrogance so infuriated a small core of Algerian intellectuals that in 1931 they formed the Association of Algerian Muslim Scholars led by Sheikh Abelhamid Ben Badis. He had received religious instruction in Tunis and Cairo, where in 1928 Hassan al Banna had launched the Muslim Brotherhood to promote Islamic reforms in Egypt.

Ben Badis framed the new movement in a few succinct words. "Islam is my religion, Arabic my language, and Algeria my country," he pronounced. With other Muslim scholars, he began preaching that Algeria could never be part of France because of its different culture, religion, and language.

Ben Badis died in 1940, fourteen years before secular Algerian nationalists launched their war for independence from France. But he is credited with spearheading the revival of Muslim and Arab identity that is a central tenet of Islamists to this day. Among his associates in the Association of Muslim Scholars were Sheikh Abdellatif Soltani (1904–1983) and Sheikh Ahmed Sahnoun (1907–2003), who began planting the seeds for the Algerian Muslim Brotherhood in 1953.

Islamic groups did not play a leadership role in Algeria's eight-year war for independence. None of the National Liberation Front's nine major leaders was an Islamist. And the war's main goals were to restore the sovereign, democratic, and social Algerian state with only a secondary reference to Islamic principles. Yet Islam was widely used to rally supporters in the rural areas. Guerrillas were called *mujahideen,* or holy warriors. And those who died for independence were dubbed *choudaha,* or religious martyrs.

After independence in July 1962, the first Algerian government under Ahmed Ben Bella lurched radically to the left, largely under the influence of

Algerian and French communists and Trotskyites, who flocked to Algiers to guide its burgeoning socialist revolution. Leftist labor union activists and Algerian communists still play an active role in politics through their own Workers' Party.

The first sign of Islamic protest surfaced in 1964 with the creation of the religious association al Qiyam, which means "Islamic values." It was led by three Islamists: Soltani, Sahnoun, and Abbasi Madani. The latter would play a major role in the Islamists' first quest for power between 1988 and 1992.

After only three years of independence, the Algerian military, led by Colonel Houari Boumediene toppled Ben Bella, threw out foreign communists, and promised a "return to the sources." Educated only in Arab countries, Boumediene promoted Islamic values, Arabic education, and Arabic culture with the help of thousands of imported Egyptian teachers, many of them Muslim Brotherhood members. But he insisted on tight state control over the process of Islamization. And he replaced communist-inspired socialism with military-backed state socialism.

Al Qiyam leaders soon had a falling out with Boumediene, particularly over their opposition to his land reform program. He banned their activities in 1966 and their organization four years later.

Boumediene's death in 1978 sparked a new phase of Islamic activism. His successor, Chadli Bendjedid, tolerated the Islamists' campaign against foreign ways, whether communism, the French language, alcohol, or Western dress for women. But the strategy soon backfired, especially on university campuses. Young Arabic-speaking Islamists found it difficult to obtain jobs because they did not speak French. Algiers even witnessed violent student clashes pitting Arabic speakers against French speakers.

The trouble came to a head in November 1982, when Islamists at the University of Algiers beheaded a leftist opponent with a sword. Bendjedid ordered the police to round up hundreds of students. In reaction, 100,000 Islamists turned out for the biggest rally ever held on the downtown Algiers campus to hear Sheikhs Soltani, Sahnoun, and Madani present a proposal to set up an Islamic state.

Madani was thrown into jail, and the other two sheikhs were placed under house arrest. The event marked a turning point in the open confrontation between Islamists and the military.

The first Islamist figure to take to the mountains to pursue an Islamic state by armed force was Mustapha Bouyali, a national liberation war veteran and visionary imam preaching at an Algiers mosque against the Western-inspired iniquities of Algerians. Bouyali launched his own holy war in early 1982 and convinced several hundred others to join his Armed Islamic Movement (MIA). Bouyali's insurrection lasted until 1987, when he was found and killed while hiding in the Algiers casbah. But the MIA lived on as an inspiration to other hardline Islamists.

Islamist influence continued to grow significantly throughout the 1980s as the military government sought to expand its popular base. Thousands of new mosques sprang up across the country, and cities and towns were given Arabic names.

In 1984, the National Assembly passed a family code based mostly on Sharia, or Islamic law. The code deprived Algerian women of many of the rights they had previous enjoyed; it also legalized polygamy. A new National Charter adopted in 1986 stressed Islam's central role in the life of the nation.

THE ALGIERS SPRING

The Islamist challenge to the military government started coming to a head during riots in Algiers in October 1988. The riots led to the collapse of Algeria's single-party system, which had been dominated by the National Liberation Front ever since independence. Islamists did not cause the riots. They were actually touched off by jobless youth and other malcontents, who attacked government buildings and offices.

Unrest then spread from the capital to other major cities. But Islamists quickly seized the turmoil to rally supporters, organize mass demonstrations, and directly challenge the military government. Shocked by the breadth and size of the burgeoning popular uprising, Bendjedid ordered the army into the cities to restore order. Estimates of the death toll from the military crackdown varied from 170 to 500.

After restoring order, Bendjedid launched a series of reforms, starting with a new constitution in early 1989 that allowed a free press and multiple political parties. In a fateful gamble, the military authorized the Islamic Salvation Front (FIS) as one of the more than fifty new parties.

The FIS's leaders were Madani, head of the defunct al Qiyam association, and Ali Belhadj, a rabble-rousing cleric from Kouba, a working-class district in downtown Algiers. Both were puritanical Salafis, but Belhadj was outspoken in his regard of manmade democracy as anathema to divine rule.

From the start, the FIS encompassed a hodgepodge of militant Islamists. They included veterans of the war in Afghanistan against the Soviet Union, known as *Algerian Afghans*; Saudi-influenced Salafis; and adherents to a homegrown school of Islamic thinking called the *Djaz'ara*.

Other more moderate Islamic parties also had their debut during this "Algiers Spring." The local branch of the Muslim Brotherhood registered as Hamas, totally unrelated to the radical Palestinian group by the same name. Algeria's Hamas was led by Sheikh Mahfoud Nahnah, who had taken over the movement after its founder, Sheikh Soltani, died in 1984.

A third Islamic party, Ennahda, was established by a highly respected scholar, Sheikh Abdallah Djaballah. He was also a Muslim Brother, although he wanted to remain independent of the Brotherhood's headquarters in Cairo.

Of the three legal Islamic parties, the radical but then nonviolent Front scored the biggest gains. In mid-1990, local elections polarized the country between Islamists and secularists when the Islamic Salvation Front won a stunning 54 percent of the vote. The ruling National Liberation Front garnered only 28 percent.

The Front captured 70 percent of the vote in the three largest cities of Algiers, Constantine, and Oran. It also swept 856 out of all 1,541 municipalities. And it gained a majority in thirty-one of the forty-eight assemblies at the *wilaya*, or provincial, level. By contrast, the Muslim Brotherhood's Ennahda Party gained only 5 percent of the popular vote.

The results put the military in a quandary about whether to go ahead with parliamentary elections. Communists, leftist labor unions, and secular parties also showed little enthusiasm as they watched the Front-dominated municipal councils demand rule under Islamic law. Front leaders Madani and Belhadj took turns threatening a holy war if elections were canceled, and they held massive rallies calling for an Islamic state. Both were arrested for promoting a nationwide strike in June 1990.

Still, the military government did hold a first round of two-part parliamentary elections on December 26, 1991. The elections confirmed the likelihood of a full Islamic Salvation Front takeover. The Front won 188 out of 231 seats compared with only 15 seats for the ruling National Liberation Front.

Secularist parties, labor unions, and women reacted by forming a National Committee for the Safeguard of Algeria. They urged the military to call off the final round of elections scheduled for January 16, 1992. So did France and the United States, which feared that, once in power, the FIS would never hold another election.

The second round was never held. Under military pressure, Bendjedid resigned on January 11, 1992. Three days later, a military-appointed State High Council took power. The opening shots of civil war rang out on February 8 during clashes between the military and Front supporters at mosques across the country. On March 4, the State High Council outlawed the Front and kept Madani and Belhadj in jail.

THE BLACK DECADE

The following eight years witnessed an ever more ruthless struggle between the military and jihadi Islamists from a plethora of armed groups. The moribund Armed Islamic Movement was revived. FIS radicals split off to form the Armed Islamic Group (GIA). The Front's more moderate members set up their own Islamic Salvation Army (AIS).

Toward the end of the 1990s, diehard Islamists opposed to all peace efforts formed the Salafist Group for Preaching and Combat (GSPC), the forerunner of the local al Qaeda branch. Tens of thousands of Afghan war veterans, jobless youth, disaffected Arabic-educated students, and plain criminals joined one of the extremist groups.

All sides participated in the bloodshed. Hallmarks of the brutal insurrection included throat-slitting and decapitation of moderate Islamists and secular intellectuals, journalists, and politicians. The disparate Islamist factions massacred each other's supporters and carried out attacks on the military. In turn, secret security force units perpetrated extrajudicial killings of even innocent villagers in a bid to discredit one Islamic group or another.

Each year, the holy month of Ramadan became a pretext for the worst slaughters. The GIA ordered all foreigners to leave the country and assassinated more than fifty who dared to stay.

The most horrific example of GIA attacks on foreigners involved the killing in May 1996 of seven Cistercian Trappist monks at the Tibhirine Monastery outside the town of Medea, which lies south of Algiers. (The 2010 film *Of Gods and Men* dramatized the event.)

The GIA even took its war to Paris, where bombs went off at subway stations and on train lines. In December 1994, four GIA terrorists hijacked an Air France civilian airliner with the intent of crashing it into the Eiffel Tower, foreshadowing tactics used in the 9/11 attacks in the United States. (The Air France hijackers were killed by French commandos while the aircraft refueled in Marseille.)

Against this backdrop of unending violence, some moderate Islamists joined secularist parties to seek a peaceful resolution of the civil war. In January 1995, two FIS leaders and Ennahda's Sheikh Djaballah joined three secular parties, including the ruling National Liberation Front, in signing a peace pact negotiated by the Rome-based Catholic Sant'Egidio Order. The Rome Accords called for a national conference to negotiate a transition back to civilian rule, the return of the army to its barracks, and an end to the ban on FIS political activities.

The military immediately rejected the accords. It instead held a presidential election to replace the military's five-member State High Council in November 1995. Islamists involved in the insurrection vehemently opposed the plan.

But the Muslim Brotherhood's Hamas opted to participate and selected its leader, Nahnah, to run against the military's General Liamine Zeroual. Nahnah captured 25 percent of the vote against Zeroual's 60 percent. As a reward for participating, the military gave Hamas two cabinet posts in the new government, which was formed on the last day of 1995.

For the first time in the history of Algeria—and the rest of North Africa—the Muslim Brotherhood had gained a foothold in government.

ISLAMISTS IN GOVERNMENT

Even in the face of escalating violence, the military next organized parliamentary elections in June 1997. This time, two Muslim Brotherhood–inspired parties agreed to participate: Hamas, now renamed the Movement of Society for Peace, and Ennahda.

The movement won 1.6 million votes, or 14.8 percent, catapulting it into the National Assembly for the first time with sixty-nine deputies. It came in second behind the National Rally for Democracy, the new government party taking over from the National Liberation Front, which captured 3.5 million votes, or 34 percent, and thus 156 seats, well short of a majority in the 380-seat assembly. Ennahda came in fourth with 915,000 votes, or 8.7 percent, giving it thirty-four seats. Together, the two moderate Islamic parties took 23.5 percent of the vote compared to only 14.3 percent for the long-ruling National Liberation Front.

Forced to form a coalition government, the military chose to include the Movement of Society for Peace in an alliance with two secular parties. This time, the MSP was put in charge of seven ministries or agencies: industry, small and medium-sized enterprises, transportation, tourism, environment, fisheries, and artisanal production. Conspicuously absent from the list was any ministry dealing with security.

The MSP has remained the principal Islamic faction supporting the military government ever since. When General Zeroual retired in 1999, the Islamist party immediately backed Abdelaziz Bouteflika, the military's choice to replace Zeroual. Since 2004, the movement has been part of a three-party alliance that repeatedly endorsed his reelection.

A national liberation war veteran and former foreign minister, Bouteflika is credited with finally ending Algeria's civil war. He first struck a peace deal with the smallest armed Islamist group, the AIS, and then offered an amnesty from prosecution to all the others. The so-called civil accord was approved in a referendum held in September 2000 by 98.6 percent of the vote, on a turnout of 85 percent.

In 2005, the civil accord was followed by the Charter for Peace and National Reconciliation, which provided compensation to the families of 25,000 victims of the civil war, including the 5,800 "disappeared," who were widely believed to be military victims. Altogether, between 100,000 and 200,000 Algerians died during the Black Decade, compared with some 1 million victims during the war for independence.

THE PRICE FOR PARTICIPATION

The MSP strategy of participation has come at considerable cost to its popularity and credibility. In the 2002 parliamentary elections, it won only a little more than 500,000 votes, or 7 percent of the total cast. Its number of deputies dropped from sixty-nine to thirty-eight. But its main Islamic rival, Ennahda, did well. Ennahda garnered 705,000 votes, or 9.5 percent, and jumped from zero to forty-three seats in the National Assembly.

In the next parliamentary elections, held in 2007, both Islamists and the military government lost legitimacy. Only 35 percent of Algeria's 18.7 million voters bothered to go to the polls. The movement won slightly more votes (552,000) than in 2002, an increase that parlayed into fifty-two seats. But Ennahda plummeted in popularity, winning fewer than 200,000 votes. The number of its deputies dropped from forty-three to just five. The Islamists combined won a mere 13 percent of the turnout.

Presidential elections in April 2009 starkly illustrated the declining popularity of both the regime and the MSP. Before the poll, Bouteflika manipulated the National Assembly to revise the constitution and allow him to run for a third term. He also engineered a successful revolt to oust Djaballah from leadership of al Islah, the party Djaballah had founded in 1999 after leaving Ennahda. This move neutralized the one Islamic opposition figure sufficiently popular to threaten Bouteflika. The MSP, however, continued to support the president.

The main question hanging over the 2009 presidential election was the turnout. Public cynicism about government manipulation of elections, parties, and poll figures reached new heights. Bouteflika was declared the winner with 90 percent of the vote, on a 75 percent turnout. The opposition, however, claimed that only 16 percent of the electorate voted.

As later disclosed in a WikiLeaks cable, the U.S. embassy in Algiers described the election as "carefully choreographed and heavily controlled" and estimated the turnout at "25 to 30 percent at most." Making the election even less representative of the political landscape, the Workers' Party's Trotskyite leader, Louisa Hanoune, came in second. The one Islamist candidate to participate received just 1 percent of the vote.

The election fallout for the Movement of Society for Peace was immediate. Within two months, a faction within the MSP led by Abdelmajid Menasra broke away to form the Movement for Preaching and Change, which criticized MSP leader Soltani for serving as a minister while also remaining party leader. Another faction that remained within the MSP felt the movement should withdraw from the government and go into open opposition. In response, Soltani resigned, but four other MSP ministers remained in the government. The military rewarded the MSP by refusing to allow the breakaway party to operate.

THE ARAB SPRING

The uprisings of early 2011 caught both the military and Algeria's Islamists by surprise. Bouteflika, at age seventy-four, had by then become an absentee president because of serious health problems. He rarely spoke in public—just three times during all of 2011. Since the president had no sons, vice president, or other obvious successor, public unease was already growing about who would lead the country next.

The political vacuum became visible when street protests over rising food prices, housing shortages, and unemployment broke out in Algiers in January 2011, sparking violent confrontations with the police. At least 3 protesters died, more than 800 others were injured, and more than 1,000 were arrested. After the mayor in another town refused him either a job or housing, an unemployed youth set himself on fire on January 13, following the model of the Tunisian street vendor whose self-immolation sparked the Arab Spring.

A secular opposition party tried repeatedly to mobilize demonstrations in Algiers, but security forces quickly quashed them. Islamists, traumatized by events during the Black Decade, were nowhere to be seen.

The government responded quickly to head off a repeat of the October 1988 riots. It was financially well placed to pacify discontent because of the country's oil wealth and high oil prices. Algeria's foreign reserves stood at $155 billion U.S. at the start of 2011 and had increased to $186 billion U.S. by September—sufficient to cover four years of imports. Food subsidies and civil servants' salaries were increased, the latter by 34 percent.

In early February, Bouteflika lifted the nineteen-year state of emergency. On April 15, he announced constitutional reforms to "strengthen democracy." They included a new media law permitting private television and radio stations, as well as a revision of the election law to allow parties to register more easily. The government also set new parliamentary elections for May 2012.

After the yearlong unrest, the MSP made its dramatic move. On New Year's Day 2012, party chief Sheikh Soltani announced the movement was quitting the three-party alliance behind President Bouteflika. Sheikh Soltani declared that 2012 would be "the year of political competition ... and not that of alliance."

Somewhat hypocritically, Soltani then denounced the coalition for "political mediocrity" that served neither the country nor its people. He also said that the MSP would keep its four ministers in the cabinet. The moves were an attempt to face the public over the movement's long record of support for the highly unpopular military but without breaking completely with the government.

KEY POSITIONS

By early 2012, Algeria had seven Islamist parties or informal factions. Three parties—Ennahda, al Islah, and the MSP—had already participated in a presidential or parliamentary election. All three were rooted in Muslim Brotherhood thinking and differed mainly over whether to seek changes in the political system from within or outside the military government.

But two of the potentially strongest Islamic contenders were not going to run in the 2012 elections. The military continued to ban the Islamic Salvation Front from politics, while the large but quiescent Salafi community showed no interest. So Algeria's active Islamist spectrum was defined by seven groups with diverse positions.

The Movement of Society for Peace

The MSP is the Islamic group that has consistently supported military rule, participation in government, and cooperation with secular parties since 1995. Its strategy has been to win more power by showing the military that it is responsible and trustworthy while gaining practical experience in governance.

Its political program carefully straddles all the hot-button issues. It avoids mention of an Islamic state or the Muslim Sharia as the law of the land. Its stated goal is a "modern Algerian state in conformity with the spirit of Islamic principles," but which also endorses democracy and "a republican regime." It recognizes the special Amazigh (Berber) origins of Algeria but also stresses that the country belongs to the Islamic and Arab worlds.

The MSP policy toward women also treads carefully. It endorses women's right to education and work, even suggesting reduced hours to allow time for raising families. But the policy does not mention revising the Islamic-inspired Family Code of 1984, and the movement has shown no support for special quotas for women in the National Assembly.

Its economic policy straddles the capitalist-socialist divide. The MSP endorses state control of "strategic public sectors" and a social welfare state including cash payments even to unemployed university graduates. But it also supports promotion of small and medium-sized private enterprises and private investment to reduce Algeria's dependence on the state-run oil sector. At the same time, it demands the creation of an Islamic banking system that forbids interest on loans.

Perhaps the most distinctive feature of the MSP's foreign policy is the prominence given to the Palestinian issue, which the movement describes as "the central cause of the nation." The MSP calls for the reconquest of "all Palestinian territory" from Israel and for an independent Palestinian state with Jerusalem as its capital. The program makes no mention of the 2002 Arab Peace Plan, which offered Israel normalization of relations in return for a resolution of the Palestinian issue.

The National Front for Change

The National Front for Change is led by Abdelmajid Menasra, who broke away from the MSP in 2009 after rejecting continued participation in government. Along with MSP leader Soltani, Menasra had been one of the first two Islamists to hold cabinet posts beginning in the mid-1990s. He subsequently became disenchanted over the lack of "real democracy" and the "empty reforms" by successive military governments. Menasra claims to have recruited away 50 percent of MSP members. His party has also called for an amnesty for former FIS members and has appealed to them to join the National Front for Change.

Menasra has said that the kind of popular uprising that occurred in Egypt and Tunisia is not the right strategy for Algerian Islamists. He has launched a petition campaign dubbed "One Million for Popular Reform" to pressure the Bouteflika regime to hold transparent elections, write a new constitution, increase freedoms, and launch new economic projects to reduce unemployment.

Ennahda

Founded by Sheikh Abdallah Djaballah in 1990, Ennahda has its roots in the Muslim Brotherhood movement. It has supported participation in the political process but not in the military government. It is not related to Tunisia's Ennahda Party and has maintained its independence from the Brotherhood's headquarters in Cairo.

In 2012, Ennahda leader Fateh Rebiai described his Islamism as "anchored in Algerian society." The party saw a sharp decline in its popularity after ousting Djaballah in 1997, who then created the rival al Islah Party. In the last parliamentary elections in 2007, Ennahda won just 3 percent of the vote and five seats. Rebiai did not compete in the 2009 presidential race.

Al Islah

Known also as the Movement for National Reform, al Islah is the successor to the nearly defunct Ennahda and was created by Abdallah Djaballah in 1999. After a dissident faction expelled Djaballah in 2006, al Islah struggled to define itself or attract support. Its leader, Mohamed Djahid Younsi, won only 177,000 votes, barely 1 percent, in the 2009 presidential election. Al Islah has since gone through several other leaders. Bouteflika adopted many of al Islah's proposed political reforms after the Arab Spring broke out in Tunisia and Egypt.

The Justice and Development Front

Launched in August 2011, the Justice and Development Front is the third party founded by Sheikh Djaballah after his ouster from both Ennahda and al Islah. A respected Islamic scholar, Djaballah is extremely conservative on social issues. His dislike of the former colonial power is such that he refuses to speak French.

Djaballah was a signatory of the 1995 Rome Accords, which rejected violence, called for national reconciliation, and recognized Islam, Arabism, and Amazigh (Berber) as central characteristics of the Algerian identity. Djaballah has prided himself on refusing to cooperate with the military regime. A highly effective orator, he probably will present the greatest challenge to both the MSP and the military regime.

The Movement for Liberty and Social Justice

Founded in 2007, this movement is led by former FIS leaders, most of whom now live in exile. They have been seeking, without success, to convince the military that their members have forsworn violence and truly embraced multiparty democracy. They claim inspiration from the Association of Algerian Muslim Scholars, which was popular in the 1930s. One of the movement's cofounders is Anwar Haddam, who was elected in 1991 to the National Assembly before the military canceled the elections. He currently lives in exile near Washington, D.C.

The movement's political platform is extremely vague. It calls simply for more freedoms, the rule of law, an end to corruption, and respect for minority and women's rights without specifics. It proclaims the need for a "realistic foreign policy" centered on cooperation with other countries of the Maghreb (Libya, Morocco, and Tunisia) and a peaceful resolution of the Palestinian problem based on a two-state solution with both entities having mixed populations of Arabs and Jews.

Salafist Group for Preaching and Combat

Founded in 1998, toward the end of the Black Decade, the GSPC broke away from the GIA with between 2,000 and 3,000 fighters. The GSPC goal is still to establish an Islamic state through force of arms. The GSPC engaged in guerrilla warfare against the army, attacks on foreigners, suicide bombings, and abduction of tourists in the Sahara Desert throughout the 2000s.

In 2006, its leader, Abdelmalek Droukdal, pledged allegiance to al Qaeda chief Osama bin Laden. Droukdal then became head of the Algerian branch of al Qaeda in the Maghreb. Only a few hundred Algerians have answered his call to jihad, which is aimed mainly against Algeria's military government. Droukdal was still alive and active in early 2012. His followers operate from bases both in the Sahara Desert and in the mountains fewer than 60 miles east of Algiers.

THE FUTURE

The military regime has regularly rigged the election process. Despite President Bouteflika's ailing health, military hardliners, known as the "eradicators" for their role in the Islamic insurgency of the 1990s, still control Algerian political life. The regime's éminence grise—General Mohammed "Toufik" Mediène, chief of the all-powerful Security and Intelligence Service since 1990—was still at his post in 2012.

The Movement of Society for Peace has boasted that it could win the 2012 election—if it were free and fair. The more realistic prognosis holds that Islamist parties could collectively win up to 35 percent of the vote. But the military is still unlikely to allow any Islamist leader to become prime minister, as had happened in neighboring Morocco and Tunisia in 2011. It had never allowed the moderate MSP to control any security ministry, even after seventeen years of serving in the government. So the Islamists might increase their presence in a new coalition government, but gaining control of power or policymaking remains a distant possibility.

Algeria seems likely to remain the one North African country under military rule despite the Arab democratic awakening of 2011.

David B. Ottaway lived in Algiers from 1962 to 1966 while working for UPI and The New York Times. *A former* Washington Post *Middle East correspondent, he coauthored with his wife, Marina,* Algeria: The Politics of a Socialist Revolution. *He visited Algeria again in 2009 and 2010 for a book about his life and times as a foreign correspondent. He is a public policy scholar at the Woodrow Wilson International Center for Scholars.*

CHAPTER 8

Syria: Old-Timers and Newcomers

Thomas Pierret

A fter years of repression, Islamist political groups reemerged in 2011 as Syria faced the most tumultuous political juncture since its independence from France in 1946. In 2011, Syria's political landscape began to be redefined by both old-timers and newcomers.

The Muslim Brotherhood was still the grandfather of Islamist politics in 2012, even though it was largely a movement of exiles bereft of any organized presence inside Syria since its failed uprising in the early 1980s. Apart from a handful of radical groups, the Brotherhood historically had few competitors on its end of the political spectrum. It played a prominent role in creating a new opposition coalition abroad after Syria's uprising began in March 2011. It was also the most influential force within the new Syrian National Council established in Istanbul in August 2011.

But the Brotherhood will not be the only Islamist movement to vie for votes in a free and fair election. It might not even be the best-placed movement to capture the support of Islamist-oriented Syrians. In December 2011, twelve members of the Syrian National Council announced the creation of the Syrian National Movement, or al Tayyar al Watani al Suri. The council vowed, like the Brotherhood, to pursue the "aims of Islam." Whether or not the council evolves into a serious rival to the Brotherhood, the newcomers embody all the challenges that the long-dominant Islamist movement will have to face in the future. The challenges are not so much ideological, since the Syrian Brotherhood boasts a long tradition of pragmatism, but instead relate to questions of age and social ties inside Syria. Most of the movement's leaders are in their forties or fifties, a generation significantly younger than their counterparts in the Brotherhood, who were already in command when the movement left Syria thirty years ago.

The Brotherhood was also largely cut off from Syrian society during those three decades, whereas many members of the movement were still based in Syria. In other words, although the Brotherhood certainly had assets—long experience in political activism, tight organization, and extensive international networks—it also had obvious handicaps, compared to the Brotherhood's new competitors.

THE BEGINNING

The Syrian branch of the Muslim Brotherhood was officially established after the withdrawal of the French colonial army from Syria in 1946. It was not a centralized movement but a national federation of preexisting local Islamic associations. The associations had been created during the previous decade by young clerics and intellectuals such as the founding superintendent, or *muraqib*, Mustafa al Sibai, a nonconformist Azharite, and Muhammad al Mubarak, an alumnus of the University of Paris. (The head of the Syrian Brotherhood is called *superintendent* because he theoretically is under the authority of the *guide*, who is the leader of the Egyptian mother organization.)

The early Syrian Brotherhood had no well-defined ideology. Its general goals were to defend Islamic norms and values against the rise of secular political forces, particularly in the realm of law. The Brotherhood also displayed striking flexibility and pragmatism from the start, however. In 1950, it lobbied for a constitutional provision that declared Islam to be "the religion of the state," but the Brotherhood eventually rallied to the majority and voted instead for a constitution stating only that the president had to be a Muslim.

The Syrian Brotherhood also adopted ideas fashionable at the time, such as Arab nationalism and socialism. In 1949, Brotherhood members ran for elections under the name Socialist Islamic Front. Ten years later, Mustafa al Sibai published his seminal work, *The Socialism of Islam*. More conservative Islamists criticized this embrace of an "imported" ideology.

Between 1949 and 1963, Syria gyrated between parliamentary and military rule because of political coups and instability. The Brotherhood, which had little influence within the military compared to its secular rivals, was committed to restoring parliamentary rule. It also enjoyed decent relations with the bourgeois nationalist parties that dominated the political landscape during Syria's so-called liberal age. Brotherhood members held ministerial positions in 1949 and 1961. In 1954, they were entrusted to establish the Faculty of Sharia at the state-run University of Damascus.

Unlike the early Egyptian Muslim Brotherhood, the Syrian branch was not a mass movement at that time. In 1961, it won its highest electoral victory with only 8.7 percent of parliamentary seats. It was actually a rather elitist organization with followers who were typically educated members of the traditional Sunni urban middle class and the sons of religious scholars, merchants, or craftsmen. It had a limited presence in rural areas. And it inevitably suffered from the political rise of the peasantry under the aegis of the Baath Party in the 1960s.

BANISHED

After the 1963 Baath Party coup, the Brotherhood faced a hostile, radically secularist regime. The movement was banned, and hundreds of its members went into exile. Among them was Isam al Attar, who succeeded Sibai as superintendent after Sibai's death in 1964. The Brotherhood operated as a semiclandestine group until the early 1980s, when it was basically eliminated inside the country.

Baathist repression also spawned frictions, which were based on regional ties that undermined the Brotherhood's unity. In the early 1970s, Attar—who had fled to Germany from his base in Damascus—was challenged by the Aleppo branch, largely because of the strength of rival regional identities. The Aleppo wing was led by Abd al Fattah Abu Ghudda, a religious scholar who was recognized by the Egyptian mother organization as the legitimate superintendent.

Prolonged military rule forced the Brotherhood to develop a new strategy. It began proselytizing systematically among the long-neglected Syrian grassroots through a network of informal study circles. By the 1970s, it was able to take advantage of the Islamic revival that swept the Muslim world and recruited a growing number of educated young people.

The Brotherhood also took advantage of a small opening shortly after President Hafez al Assad seized power in a bloodless coup in 1970. Assad allowed conservative candidates backed by the Brotherhood to run for office and to win seats both on local councils and, to a lesser extent, in parliament.

But old tensions reemerged in the late 1970s as the Assad regime grew increasingly unpopular. The Brotherhood also elected a new superintendent, Adnan Sa'd al Din, from the hardline faction in the central city of Hama. Syria's main Islamist group decided it was no longer willing to work within a system of "liberalized authoritarianism." It joined secular parties in boycotting the 1977 elections.

ARMED STRUGGLE

The confrontation eventually degenerated into armed struggle. Young Brotherhood activists had initially taken up arms in Hama in 1964, but they were easily suppressed by the regime and subsequently disavowed by their own leadership. The radical cell was led by Said Hawwa, a Sharia graduate who later became a prominent Brotherhood ideologue, and Marwan Hadid, an engineer who eventually split from the organization as a result of its passivity.

After Hadid's death in prison, his followers formed the Fighting Vanguard, or al Tali'a al Muqatila, and launched a campaign to assassinate state officials. In 1979, its massacre of dozens of Alawite cadets in the Artillery School of Aleppo plunged the country into turmoil. Popular uprisings erupted in the northern cities as large numbers of young people joined the Fighting Vanguard.

During the early months of the uprising, the Brotherhood initially negotiated with the regime, even securing the release of hundreds of its followers in early 1980s. But the regime launched a bloody crackdown as popular protests escalated. In June 1980, military units, led by President Assad's brother Rifaat, executed some 1,000 Islamists detained in a Palmyra prison to retaliate for a failed assassination attempt against the president. The regime then passed Law 49, which made membership in the Brotherhood a capital offense.

The Brotherhood's attacks against the regime were far less effective than attacks by the Fighting Vanguard, which continued to carry out most of the assassinations and bombings. The Brotherhood had more influence outside Syria in generating media and political attention. Its propaganda sometimes had sectarian, anti-Alawite overtones, but its political objectives were unchanged. Its 1980 political program defined the ideal political system as a combination of liberal institutions and Islamic laws.

The denouement in the Islamist uprising played out in Hama, Syria's third-largest city, in February 1982. The Assad regime responded by crushing the armed insurgency with heavy artillery bombardment and mass killings. The death toll was estimated at between 10,000 and 25,000. By the mid-1980s, both the Brotherhood and the Fighting Vanguard networks were completely destroyed. The Vanguard ceased to exist, whereas the Brotherhood remained active in exile even though it was riven by splits between its Aleppo and Hama factions between 1986 and 1992.

IN EXILE

With no prospects of toppling the regime, the Brotherhood's main concern was retaining political relevance. In 1985, it agreed to meet Syrian security officials in Germany, but the talks ended in failure. In 1995, former Superintendent Abu Ghudda was allowed to visit Syria, but his request to meet with President Assad was ignored. More promising discussions were held in 1999, but they ended abruptly after the assassination in Aleppo of the go-between, Amin Yakan, a prominent former Brotherhood member.

During the same period, the Islamist group established parallel ties with the secular opposition. In 1982, it joined with the pro-Iraq wing of the Baath Party to form the National Alliance for the Liberation of Syria. The coalition lasted for a decade before disintegrating. The Brotherhood did not try again to unify the opposition until the presidential succession—when Hafez al Assad died and was replaced as president by his son Bashar al Assad in 2000—revived hopes for political reforms in Syria.

In 2001, two years after a Syrian-Jordanian rapprochement forced it to move its headquarters from Amman to London, the Brotherhood published the *National Honor Pact*. The document formally rejected the use of violence and called for dialogue among all Syrian political forces. The next year, the Brotherhood organized a National Dialogue conference in London, although neither the regime nor other opposition groups expressed serious interest in attending.

The Brotherhood began to be taken more seriously by interlocutors after the U.S. invasion of Iraq in 2003, which at least initially also left Syria feeling more vulnerable. The group sent positive signals to the regime, including a call by Superintendent Ali Sadr al Din al Bayanuni for a comprehensive national reconciliation. Indirect contacts between the Brotherhood and the Assad regime resumed through foreign Islamists over the next few months.

In 2004, United Nations Resolution 1559 increased international pressure on Damascus by calling for withdrawal of all Syrian forces from Lebanon. The Brotherhood, in turn, became more assertive. Three months later, it released the Political Project for Future Syria, its first detailed political program since 1980. The new project called for a regime that would be "republican and democratic" with liberal institutions but also "Islamic" because its constitution would make Islam the "religion of the state" and laws would be "gradually Islamized."

THE DAMASCUS DECLARATION

The assassination of former Lebanese Prime Minister Rafik Hariri in February 2005 dramatically affected Syria too. Lebanese protests forced Syria to withdraw its army after a twenty-nine-year occupation.

The shifting political tide allowed the Brotherhood to make spectacular inroads in rapprochement with secular opposition groups. It agreed to join the Damascus Declaration for Democratic Change, a broad alliance of political forces launched in October 2005. Joining forces with mainstream secular activists such as Michel Kilo was a major achievement for a movement demonized by state propaganda and feared by secular groups for the previous quarter-century. In 2005, the Brotherhood's truce with the regime also collapsed when President Assad refused to follow through on promised political reforms.

But the Brotherhood also soon miscalculated its position. In March 2006, Bayanuni and former Syrian Vice President Abd al Halim Khaddam, who had just defected, announced the creation of the National Salvation Front. This was an odd move for the Brotherhood. It forced a de facto break with members of the Damascus Declaration.

Khaddam was also far from being the right horse to back, despite his former position. He was perceived in Syria as one of the regime's most corrupt figures. He had been marginalized for several years, leaving him little leverage inside the state apparatus. By the time the Front was created, the regime had also survived the most difficult phase of the Lebanese crisis. The Front emerged too late to capitalize on the political drama.

In 2009, the Brotherhood broke from the Front after the Gaza war between Israel and Hamas. It also announced a unilateral truce with the Assad regime, after which Damascus signaled it was ready to resume talks. The regime did not, however, follow through by lifting Law 49, which carried the death penalty for membership in the Brotherhood.

LEADERSHIP CHANGE

The setback led to a major leadership change. In 2010, the Aleppo faction lost out to the Hama faction in the Brotherhood's internal elections. Bayanuni, who finished his third and final term, was replaced by Riyad Shuqfe as the new superintendent. Shuqfe, who had led the Brotherhood's military unit in the early 1980s, was considered a hardliner. He opposed the group's unilateral truce; he was about to ask the Consultative Council to renounce the truce when uprisings erupted in Tunisia and Egypt.

After Syrian protesters launched their own uprising in March 2011, the exiled Brotherhood leadership had little influence over the situation on the ground. But the Brotherhood did play a leading role in assembling the opposition abroad to establish the Syrian National Council in August 2011.

With about one-quarter of the council seats, the Brotherhood holds the largest representation. Yet in a sign of the newcomers' clout, the Brotherhood only holds about one-half of the total number of Islamist seats within the council. In early 2012, the rest were in the hands of recently exiled clerics and, more important, the recently founded movements.

OTHER GROUPS

Apart from radical groups, such as the Fighting Vanguard or shadowy Salafi networks, the Syrian Brotherhood historically had one main Islamist challenger—the Islamic Liberation Party, or Hizb al Tahrir al Islami. The underground cultlike but nonviolent organization was created in Palestine in 1953. It promoted the immediate restoration of the caliphate and rejected any participation in existing political systems. Its members are estimated to number only in the hundreds. They have reportedly participated in the present uprising, but are not represented on the Syrian National Council.

But more pragmatic competitors have emerged in recent years. The Movement for Justice and Development (MJD), or Harakat al Adala wal Bina, was founded in London in 2006 by geologist Anas al Abda and economist Osama al Munajjid (who left the MJD in 2010). It was created a few weeks after the formation of the National Salvation Front; it effectively replaced the Brotherhood as the Islamist branch of the Damascus Declaration.

The MJD distinguishes itself from the Brotherhood by promoting a post-Islamist identity. The name of the movement and its ideology are both inspired by the ruling Turkish Justice and Development Party. Its program calls for a constitution that declares Syria a country of "Islamic civilization and culture," but it makes no reference to the concept of an Islamic state or to implementation of Sharia. Moreover, the "people's will" is presented as the only source of laws. The MJD is represented on the Syrian National Council.

The Syrian National Movement is not a formal party but an umbrella for five different groups: liberal Islamists, members of mosque-based educational groups, Salafis, secular liberals based in the West, and left-wing secularists based in Syria. The common ground is acceptance of the "Islamic reference," or *al marja'iyya al Islamiyya*, whether as a source of legislation for Islamists or as the cultural and civilizational identity of Syria for secularists.

The Syrian National Movement emphasizes that it is not a group of exiles with few ties to Syrian society—unlike the Brotherhood and the MJD. Two-thirds of the thirty-five founding members still live in Syria, but those who sit on the Syrian National Council left the country in 2011. Its president is Imad al Din al Rashid, the former vice dean of the Faculty of Sharia of Damascus University. He did not go into exile until the spring of 2011.

Other Islamic-oriented activists have joined the National Action Group, or Majmu'at al Amal al Watani. It has representation on the Syrian National Council. Outside the council, Luay al Zobi, a Salafi who is based in Lebanon, has given interviews in which he presents himself as the head of a so far mysterious movement called the Believers Participate, or Al Mu'minun Yusharikun.

KEY POSITIONS

The ideology of the Syrian Brotherhood has changed relatively little since 1946, reflecting that its ideology was relatively flexible and pragmatic from the start.

Islam and Democracy

In its 2004 program, the Brotherhood stated clearly that it had not given up the goal of establishing an "Islamic state" through the "gradual Islamization of laws." But it called its ideal state "civilian" and not theocratic. Indeed, it said that the government should be formed by and be accountable to a parliament that is renewed regularly through multiparty elections. At the same time, the Brotherhood's political program also sought to give an undefined role to unelected "specialists" in the elaboration of laws, which could provide a basis for involving religious scholars in the legislative process.

Women's Rights

On personal status law, the Brotherhood is not willing to fundamentally challenge the Sharia-based legal framework in Syria. On social and political rights, the 2004 document stated that "it is not forbidden for a woman to become a judge, an administrator, or a minister." The group encourages women to dress "modestly" without specifying if the dress code should be enforced by the state.

Religious Minorities

The Brotherhood does not seek to change Syria's existing personal status law for Christians, which grants them significant autonomy. In terms of political rights, the Brotherhood cites statements made by founder Mustafa al Sibai in front of the Syrian parliament in 1950. "Citizens are equal in terms of rights," he said. "None should be prevented from occupying the highest positions in the state because of his religion, gender, or language." Brotherhood officials have stated on several occasions that they would be ready to accept the election of an Alawite or a Christian as head of the state.

Ethnic Minorities

The issue of ethnic minorities is theoretically less problematic than that of religious minorities, because the largest share of Syrian ethnic minorities (Kurds, Turkmens, and Circassians) are Sunni Muslims. But some opposition Kurds have complained about the group's insistence on the Arab identity of Syria and opposition to Kurdish self-determination.

The United States and the West

The Brotherhood is not fundamentally hostile to the West, partly because much of its leadership is based in Western countries and partly because it opposes a regime that has traditionally had tense relations with the West. Its 2004 political program even called the West "the free world." But the Brotherhood has criticized the U.S. invasion of Iraq and America's "unlimited" support for Israel.

Israel

The Brotherhood does not officially recognize Israel. Its program seeks to "counter the Zionist project in its different aspects"—a position unlikely to change before an Israeli withdrawal from the Golan Heights. The group has also traditionally supported Hamas, the Palestinian Islamist movement that also emerged from Egypt's Muslim Brotherhood. There have been some tensions between the two groups since the Syrian uprising began in March 2011.

THE OTHER GROUPS' POSITIONS

The other Syrian Islamist movements have not released detailed political programs. The main difference between the MJD and the Brotherhood is that the newer MJD does not call for either an Islamic state or the Islamization of laws. The MJD defines the "people's will" as the only source of legislation. Its positions on women and minorities are thus likely to be even more flexible. Since its foundation, the MJD has been highly proactive in establishing ties with Western governments.

The Syrian National Movement is ideologically heterogeneous; it does not propose a unified vision of social and political issues. Nevertheless, it stresses the importance of equal citizenship for all Syrians in the framework of the "Islamic reference," which is broadly defined as a civilizational and cultural identity.

After the uprising began in 2011, the Brotherhood and the MJD favored creation of a no-fly zone, possibly enforced by Western air forces. But the Syrian National Movement has strongly resisted foreign military involvement in order to maintain Syria's independence. It has instead advocated logistical support for the Free Syrian Army.

THE FUTURE

In a postrevolutionary Syria, Islamists would necessarily be faced with difficult choices, particularly on legislation. The Brotherhood and some members of the newer Syrian National Movement favor the Islamization of laws in principle. But actually pushing for Islamic law could endanger their partnerships with secular and non-Sunni Muslim political forces as well as with the West.

But the Islamist movements may face far tougher hurdles first. A new government may have to reconstruct a state seriously damaged by the uprising. The current opposition, especially the exiles, would have to build a popular base almost from scratch—particularly among the Local Coordination Committees and the Free Syrian Army brigades that have carried out the uprising.

On economic issues, the Brotherhood's strong pro-market approach may pit it against the demands of the working class and peasants, who have provided the sheer bulk of demonstrators since March 2011.

The post-Assad Islamist scene is also likely to be fragmented. The Brotherhood and the MJD would probably have to compete or ally with groups more grounded inside Syria, such as the Syrian National Movement, or other Islamic forces that are locally rooted but are not politically organized at the moment, such as the *ulema* (religious scholars), the Sufi brotherhoods, the Salafis, or the Islamic Liberation Party.

Islamists would also face serious dilemmas on foreign policy. They would generally want to balance good relations with the West, in order to get economic support, with a nationalist agenda opposing Israel's occupation of the Golan Heights and the Palestinian Occupied Territories. Severing ties with Iran and Hezbollah might be a less painful choice, given the widespread popular resentment of the Assad regime's two foremost supporters.

In the near future, the question of the Islamists' ideological influence on legislation, women's rights, minority rights, and foreign policy options will almost certainly be secondary to more crucial issues, including existential issues regarding whether Syria can survive as a unified country.

Thomas Pierret is a lecturer in contemporary Islam at the University of Edinburgh. He is the author of Baas et Islam en Syrie *(2011); the English version, titled* Religion and State in Syria*, will be published by Cambridge University Press. His blog in French is http://blogs.mediapart.fr/blog/Thomas%20 Pierret.*

CHAPTER 9

The Palestinians: Fighting and Governing

Nathan J. Brown

I n a landmark 2006 election, the Palestinians rejected the long-standing political status quo and turned over power to Islamists through the ballot box. It was a stunning upset. Hamas trumped Fatah, the party of Yasser Arafat, which had dominated Palestinian political life for almost a half-century. Even Hamas was surprised by the outcome. The victory of an Islamist party had a wide-ranging effect on both the Palestinian Authority (PA) and the greater Middle East.

The breakthrough was not expected to happen that way. Hamas, an offshoot of the Muslim Brotherhood, made the strategic decision in 2006 to run for the first time. It expected to win a fair share of seats and then lead the opposition from inside the system. Fatah calculated that the shift would integrate its primary opposition into the system but under its control. Even Palestinian pollsters predicted that Fatah would win a majority and continue to govern the not-quite-state.

Instead, Hamas won an outright majority. It abruptly had to shift from being an underground movement to running government ministries and a parliament. The transformation has been one of the most profound in Islamist politics. Hamas—formally known as the Movement of Islamic Resistance—had emerged from roots in the Muslim Brotherhood. It was dedicated to providing Palestinians with an alternative to the secular and nationalist movements.

Hamas was also designed to show not only that Islamists were concerned with prayer and religious practice but also that they could actively defend Palestinian interests by force of arms. After mainstream Palestinian leaders embarked on a peace process with Israel in the 1990s, Hamas stood outside and insisted on continuing "resistance" in all forms—including attacks on Israeli civilians.

So when it won the 2006 elections, Hamas had to figure out how to be a resistance organization, a religious movement, and a governing party all at the same time. Its task was made more difficult by a cutoff of funds from the international community and diplomatic isolation. A year after Hamas's victory, a brief civil war split the PA into its two geographic parts. Hamas emerged in uncontested control of Gaza, but it was tossed out of power and driven partly back underground in the West Bank.

Western countries, led by the United States, spearheaded an effort to outmaneuver Hamas, isolate it, and even oust it from power. As an alternative, they provided diplomatic and financial support to the West Bank government headed by President Mahmoud Abbas of Fatah and Prime Minister Salam Fayyad, a technocrat. By 2012, however, Hamas was neither contained nor forced out of power; it was deeply entrenched in Gaza and could watch with some comfort as its Islamist allies seemed to be growing in strength across the region.

THE BEGINNING

Hamas constantly boasts that it grew out of the remnants of the Palestinian Muslim Brotherhood. The Egyptian Brotherhood had encouraged Palestinians to form their own chapter while Palestine was under British Mandate. In 1948, when the British withdrew from Palestine, the Egyptian Brotherhood mobilized followers to support the Palestinians in the war against the Zionist movement. The war ended with Israel's creation on more than three-quarters of the territory of Palestine.

The bitter defeat meant dispersal for the Palestinian Brotherhood; its remnants were too discouraged to undertake political activity for many years. Some in the West Bank joined the Jordanian Brotherhood. (Jordan annexed the West Bank and controlled it in the wake of the 1948 war until 1967.) Palestinians in Gaza had little freedom to maneuver because, until 1967, they were under control of an Egyptian regime hostile to the Brotherhood.

Some Palestinian Islamists who had migrated outside of Palestine— especially to other Arab countries—tried to organize independently. But most first gravitated to Fatah, a movement that actually had many former Brotherhood members among its founders.

The 1967 war brought the West Bank and Gaza under Israeli control. The Brotherhood's political positions were hardly friendly to Israel's policy—or even Israel's existence. But the movement's insistence that Palestine had to become more Islamic before it was liberated seemed a welcome gift to Israeli security officials, who allowed the Islamists some freedom to pursue their social and religious activities.

As a result, tensions deepened among Palestinian groups in the 1970s and 1980s. Other Palestinian movements criticized the Brotherhood for abandoning politics. In turn, Islamists were repelled by the collection of leftist and nationalist ideologies prevailing in Palestinian resistance circles. When Islamists became active, their goal was often as much to contest the local influence of non-Islamist groups as to resist Israel. The bitter rivalry led to intense, occasionally even physical battles for control of organizations as well as Palestinian loyalties.

ISRAEL'S ROLE

Over time, Israel's decision to use the Islamists as a counterweight to resistance groups gradually helped the Brotherhood breed a new generation of activists who pushed to move beyond religion and use social activities as the base for politics. At the same time, a new generation of Palestinian leaders also emerged in Kuwait, Jordan, and Egypt to generate momentum behind Islamists joining the resistance.

By the late 1980s, the disparate efforts coalesced to launch the Islamic Resistance Movement—or Hamas, its Arabic acronym—to ensure the presence of an Islamist participant in the Palestinian struggle. The new movement was most visible in Gaza, but West Bank Islamists joined in early as well. Hamas formally announced its existence when the first Palestinian uprising, or Intifada, erupted against Israeli occupation in 1987.

Over the next few years, Hamas led major attacks against Israeli targets, transforming the relationship. Israeli occupation authorities, who had viewed the Islamist movement as a quiescent alternative to nationalists and leftists, suddenly confronted the reality of an armed, militant, and well-organized opposition willing to use religion to justify violence. And attempts to crush the organization through arrests, detentions, and expulsions were decidedly unsuccessful.

The underground resistance organization also soon became far more politically active—and powerful—than the Brotherhood that had spawned it. The decision to engage in both politics and armed action came at a time that other Islamist groups in the Arab world were also stepping up political involvement. Hamas's founders may have been influenced by this trend. But they may also have been inspired by the 1979 Iranian Revolution. Iran was hardly a political model, but the idea of an Islamic-flavored revolutionary movement inspired some Palestinians.

A MILITANT WING

Unlike other Brotherhood movements that tried to operate through legal channels where possible, Hamas totally rejected the Israeli occupation and demonstrated no qualms about using violence. In the 1980s, Israel's arrests of Hamas leaders led the movement to create a clandestine military wing. The various branches of Hamas—which was by now part social movement, part militia, and part political party and was spread throughout the West Bank, Gaza, and the Diaspora—coordinated remarkably well, given the geographic separation and diverse priorities. The various wings of Hamas—political, social service, and military—worked hard to coordinate while maintaining their separate priorities.

By the late 1980s, Hamas had sufficient standing that it was a serious alternative to the long-dominant nationalist and leftist factions. The Islamist group did not reject cooperation with other movements. But its terms for joining the Palestine Liberation Organization (PLO)—the umbrella organization then gaining international acceptance as the sole legitimate representative of the Palestinian people—included a large representation in all PLO bodies. The price proved too high for the PLO leadership. But Hamas made inroads in all other parts of Palestinian society, from universities to the refugee camps.

During this phase, the political positions of Hamas remained uncompromising. It insisted that Palestine should be liberated from the river to the sea—meaning it refused to recognize Israel. Armed struggle was justified to attain that end.

Hamas showed some signs of flexibility, although whether this flexibility was tactical or a real hint of moderation was always unclear—and leaders themselves probably differed. Hamas did offer, for instance, to negotiate a truce of defined duration with Israel. And it suggested at times that it would accept a Palestinian state limited to the West Bank and Gaza as long as it did not have to recognize Israel.

THE PEACE PROCESS

In 1993, the Oslo Accords signed by PLO leader Yasser Arafat dramatically altered the political environment for Hamas. The agreement between the PLO and Israel created the Palestinian Authority to govern civil and security affairs of parts of the West Bank and Gaza. The PA created ministries, wrote laws, and drafted a constitutional framework as the basis of an eventual Palestinian state. In 1996, it held the first presidential and parliamentary elections.

During this second phase, Hamas joined smaller Palestinian factions in rejecting the Oslo Accords. It declared that the Israeli occupation had not ended, so neither would the resistance. Indeed, in the early Oslo period, Hamas increased attacks on Israeli civilians, especially after the massacre of Palestinian worshippers by an Israeli settler in Hebron in 1994.

But Hamas could not ignore the challenges posed by the Palestinian Authority. It clashed with the new Palestinian security forces. Under heavy pressure from Israel and the United States to gain control, the PA tried to squeeze Hamas, especially after Hamas's bombing campaign of 1994.

The Palestinian Authority also established patronage that obscured distinctions between institutions of the proto-state and Arafat's personal political machine in Fatah, which left Hamas (somewhat willingly, perhaps) out in the cold. Hamas faced profound short-term challenges as the PA won an initial burst of popular support simply through the prospect of statehood, even as it moved against other Palestinians in Hamas.

The peace process offered some opportunities for Hamas, however. As daily management of civil affairs in the West Bank and Gaza passed from Israeli to Palestinian hands, Hamas gained a bit more freedom to maneuver, especially in nonpolitical affairs and social services. In contrast, the PA's standing in Palestinian society sometimes placed limits on what PA security officials felt comfortable doing.

THE FIRST ELECTIONS

Palestinian elections posed a particularly vexing issue for Hamas. The movement was anxious to prove its popular standing but also to withhold its blessing from any part of the Oslo process.

After a series of internal debates throughout the 1990s, Hamas leaders made four basic shifts. First, they declared that they wanted no part of violence among Palestinians and would therefore react with restraint to PA forces. The one major caveat was that Hamas followers would defend themselves if forced to do so. Hamas largely held to this stance, even when its leaders and followers were arrested and tortured.

Second, after some hesitation, the movement decided not to enter the 1996 parliamentary and presidential elections. A splinter Hamas group did run candidates, scoring modest successes. Although they stayed away from national elections, Hamas leaders suggested that they might run in local elections—a stand that made Fatah repeatedly postpone the polls.

Third, the movement generally scaled back its "resistance," anxious not to provoke PA repression or popular ire as a result of the harsh Israeli countermeasures. Finally, Islamists in general turned their emphasis from the political sphere—where the cards were temporarily stacked against them—to social, educational, and charitable work.

Hamas also softened some of its positions on political issues, although gradually. The language used by key leaders became less religious and more political. (As long as Hamas's opposition to Israel was framed in religious terms, compromise was difficult.)

The second intifada in 2000 constituted a turning point as pivotal as the Oslo Accords. "Resistance" was suddenly the common denominator for all Palestinian groups, and Hamas seized a leadership role. In response, Israel escalated its own campaign, including the assassination of several Hamas leaders. But Hamas's ability to operate independently of the skills or charisma of particular individuals paid off handsomely. The elimination of senior officials seemed to leave no permanent scar on Hamas's capabilities.

After the second intifada, Hamas emerged with enhanced political credentials. The organization was far healthier than any of its rivals. And it had avoided being tainted by association with the Palestinian Authority, which was widely seen as not only irrelevant and impotent but venal as well.

THE 2006 ELECTION

By 2006, Hamas had a hard-earned if bloody reputation for promoting the Palestinian cause. Fatah, by contrast, was associated with decay, corruption, and infighting. Both factors contributed to Hamas's stunning upset in the January parliamentary elections. Fatah also sabotaged its own prospects by running too many candidates, who ended up taking votes away from each other.

Unprepared for its sudden electoral success, Hamas tried to form a coalition government, but other parties balked. International actors, led by the United States, refused to transfer vital assistance to the new government unless it immediately accepted specific conditions, including renouncing violence and accepting the binding nature of past agreements. Israel, which collected taxes for the PA, also refused to turn over revenue to the Hamas government. And Fatah, which still controlled the PA presidency, the bureaucracy, and the security services, sought to undermine Hamas through any means possible, including strikes and threats of dissolving the new parliament.

So Hamas first had to go into the government alone. It faced international boycotts, fiscal strangulation, and strikes by government workers, but it held firm. A national unity government between Fatah and Hamas was briefly brokered in early 2007, but by the spring intermittent violence erupted between the two groups, especially in Gaza. As Egypt, Jordan, and the United States provided material support to forces under Fatah control, Hamas moved against security forces under Fatah's control in Gaza.

Gaza's brief and brutal civil war in 2007 was mirrored in the West Bank, where President Mahmoud Abbas fired the Hamas-led government and replaced it with technocrats. The West Bank leadership sought to purge Hamas supporters from public institutions in the West Bank, while Hamas moved against Fatah in Gaza.

THREE BIG ISSUES

The tensions presented Hamas with difficult choices. Its platform pledged to reform Palestinian society along Islamic lines, to resist Israel, and to provide viable government. But since 2007, Hamas has struggled over which path to emphasize.

The first path emphasizes the group's Islamist agenda. Since its founding in Egypt in 1928, the Muslim Brotherhood has always emphasized reforming the individual and the society along Islamic lines. But to win the 2006 elections, Hamas downplayed Islam. It focused on promoting political reform and ending corruption rather than on a specific religious agenda.

After 2007, however, some Hamas activists sought to use the movement's ascendance to bring Palestine's legal framework and public life into line with Islamic values and teachings. The activists were generally held back by the Hamas leadership, which gave priority to political and governance issues. But in 2012, Hamas moved to rebuild a broader Muslim Brotherhood organization, which may mean some return to a religious agenda for some parts of the movement.

The second path for Hamas emphasizes resistance, literally the movement's middle name. Yet as with the Islamist agenda of Hamas, its pursuit of resistance has been uneven since 2007. It fired rockets from Gaza—but with the declared aim of securing a cease-fire with Israel on more favorable terms. And when an indirectly negotiated cease-fire did take hold, Hamas largely observed it and even enforced it on other factions.

Hamas's third path is governing, the preferred course of action for a normal political party. But Hamas has not seen itself as a normal political party. Leaders present the movement as the "un-Fatah" in every respect. Fatah had become mired in corruption, unwilling to share political power, and unable to protect the Palestinian Authority against Israeli assault. Fatah leaders showed a proclivity for writing laws and then violating them when they did not suit Fatah's needs.

Hamas promised in 2006 to take a different path: it would reluctantly govern, but it would distinguish between party and government. But it, too, abandoned its pledge after seizing power in Gaza in June 2007. No longer the un-Fatah, Hamas harassed political opponents, sought to control nongovernmental organizations, and bent the law. It also had its own scandals.

Oddly, for an ideological movement, Hamas has been fairly short on specifics on either a political program or basic issues. Leaders often cite two core ideological documents, but neither seems to guide the movement in practice.

The Hamas charter from the late 1980s is a hodgepodge of blustering, militant positions, and conspiracy theories, edging at times into anti-Semitism. The charter is almost never mentioned by movement members, some of whom seem embarrassed by its contents. The second document is the platform from the 2006 elections, which is far more restrained and focuses on issues of governance and political reform. After 2006, Hamas members of parliament and ministers often cited it as almost a contract with Palestinian voters. But its contents have largely been forgotten since the Palestinian split in 2007.

KEY POSITIONS

The general positions of Hamas are broad and sometimes ill defined.

Israel

The movement is at its most loquacious on issues involving the struggle with Israel, but there is vagueness even here. Hamas has clearly stated that it does not accept Israel. But it will accept a Palestinian state on the 1967 borders. Precisely what will be on the far side of that border is unclear. Hamas has hinted that it might reach a modus vivendi with Israel. It has also suggested that it might abide by a Palestinian peace agreement with Israel, even if the movement itself opposes that agreement. But these are mere hints, and individual Hamas leaders sometimes seem to differ on where they stand.

Democracy

Democracy did not play much of a role in the group's early thinking, but Hamas does claim to internally follow democratic procedures. In the 1990s, while it was repressed by the PA, Hamas also began to emphasize human rights and rule of law.

Hamas's 2006 electoral triumph increased its rhetorical commitment to democracy. In 2012, however, its leaders seem to want decision making by consensus among Palestinians rather than democratic vote. Like many political actors, Hamas's enthusiasm for elections waxes and wanes with the group's standing in the polls.

Islam

Hamas is unquestionably Islamic in orientation, but it also describes itself as a *wasatiyya*, or centrist, movement dedicated to moderation, flexibility, and gradualism in applying Islamic norms to public life. That description gives its positions a socially conservative flavor, but Hamas is generally willing to admit a wide variety of interpretations and postpone demands to apply Islamic law in the short term.

THE FUTURE

For the Islamic Resistance Movement, putting governance above Islam and resistance may seem a surprising choice. Hamas's leaders seem to want to show that they can rule Gaza efficiently and pursue international diplomacy even if it means postponing other parts of the group's mission. But ruling Gaza is clearly not the organization's ultimate goal.

One year after the Egyptian revolution, Hamas took small steps toward expanding its horizons, partly to take advantage of the West Bank leaders' failure to achieve any progress on peace with Israel and partly to exploit a regional climate more conducive to Islamist parties. Hamas leaders toned down their ideological rhetoric. They moved to reconcile with Fatah. And they sent officials on regional diplomatic trips.

Hamas also announced an intention to build a comprehensive Muslim Brotherhood organization. Its precise plan is not yet completely clear, but it would have three significant long-term implications. First, it could lead to a shift of focus among Palestinian Islamists. Hamas has stressed resistance. But Brotherhood organizations portray themselves as more comprehensive, with religious, personal, educational, social, charitable, and political dimensions. Second, chains of command within the organization may shift. In 2012, three parts of the movement—the Hamas-led government in Gaza, a military wing, and a leadership in the diaspora—were all vying for influence. Forming a more hierarchical movement with a general supervisor, as in other Brotherhood movements, might shift power within the movement. And third, the Palestinian Brotherhood might seek to mimic the behavior of successful Islamist movements in North Africa, which have achieved unprecedented electoral success by emphasizing gradual political reform and soothing rhetoric.

Nathan J. Brown is professor of political science and international affairs at George Washington University. He is also a nonresident senior associate of the Carnegie Endowment for International Peace. His most recent book is When Victory Is Not an Option: Islamist Movements in Arab Politics *(2012). His website is http://home.gwu.edu/~nbrown.*

CHAPTER 10

Morocco: The King's Islamists

Abdeslam Maghraoui

In a microcosm of the Arab world's new political spectrum, Morocco now has two rival Islamist powers—one that dominates government and the other that is a banned but popular opposition group. The monarchy, however, still has ultimate control and effective veto power over the political realm. King Mohammed VI tolerated the rise of an Islamist party partly in response to the same kind of demands for reform that have swept North Africa. But Morocco's experiment also has unique characteristics that are separate from the Arab Spring.

The Justice and Development Party (PJD), which has been the leading Islamist party since 1998, won the right to form a government after winning 27 percent of the vote in the November 2011 parliamentary elections. It is a politically moderate but socially conservative party. The king appointed Abdelilah Benkirane, the party's general secretary, to form a power-sharing coalition government in January 2012. Members of the politically moderate Islamist party gained control of important ministries, including the ministries of higher education, justice, and foreign affairs.

The main Islamist opposition in Morocco is Justice and Charity, a grassroots movement founded in 1987 by Sheikh Abdessalam Yassin, a charismatic leader and member of a Sufi order. Unlike the PJD, Justice and Charity refuses to participate in the political system under conditions it considers illegitimate. It also rejects the dual authority of the king as both head of state and as commander of the faithful, or *Amir al Mouminin*. Justice and Charity has, in turn, been banned from politics.

The rise of the Justice and Development Party is significant for three reasons. First, the formation of an Islamist government in 2012 was only the second time since independence in 1956 that the monarchy allowed an alternation of power. The king also agreed to reforms that give him less control over government—notably, choosing the prime minister from the party with the largest number of seats in parliament.

Second, an Islamist-led government could erode the monarchy's tattered religious legitimacy if the PJD projects a socially progressive political agenda and relegates doctrinal disputes to the official religious establishment. Finally, an Islamist government could complicate Morocco's solid strategic relations with Western powers.

Yet beyond symbolic gestures, the prospects of significant political change under the new government are realistically close to nil. Moroccan Islamists clearly benefited from protests and pressure unleashed by the February 20 movement, a Moroccan version of the Arab protest movements. Subsequent constitutional amendments gave the government more powers. But the PJD's political ascendance is in no way comparable to the mass electoral victories and popular mandates of Islamists in Egypt and Tunisia.

The PJD was basically domesticated by the palace before it was first allowed to participate in local and legislative elections in 1997. The monarchy's formal powers and informal networks also remain as strong and extensive as ever. In 2012, the monarchy played a behind-the-scenes role in identifying—and vetoing—cabinet members for sensitive posts. Before the new government was even formed, the king hired key figures from the previous cabinet as counselors, who will have significant executive power and influence.

Finally, the Justice and Development Party has not made a clear commitment to modern universal principles to qualify as the Muslim democratic force it claims to be. On many crucial issues—including women's rights, cultural openness and diversity, freedom of expression, and rights of non-Arab Amazigh (Berber) people—the PJD is lagging behind both the monarchy and the banned Islamist movement Justice and Charity.

THE BEGINNING

The PJD's birth took a long political and ideological detour that illustrates the challenge often facing Islamists under authoritarian rule: they can accept political co-optation and risk losing their popular legitimacy, or they can remain in the opposition but risk ideological radicalization. The PJD took the route of moderation and co-optation. It was part of the monarchy's effort to create a counterweight to the uncompromising Justice and Charity and an increasingly assertive secular civil society.

The PJD's leadership is generally younger and more collegial than their counterparts in Justice and Charity. Born in 1954, Abdelilah Benkirane was a member of Muslim Youths (Chabiba al Islamiya), a radical clandestine movement established in 1969. The movement's leader, Abdelkrim Mouti, an inspector of primary education, was influenced by the writings of radical Egyptian Islamist Sayyid Qutb. The group's original target was universities, which were then under the sway of secular leftists. The PJD's main objective was to liberate society from *jahiliya*, which refers to ignorance of divine guidance in pre-Islamic Arabia.

The monarchy's tolerance of Muslim Youths began to wane after the group's assassination of a leftist labor leader in 1975 and Iran's Islamic revolution in 1979. In the late 1970s and early 1980s, the government launched a dual strategy of repression and co-optation of Islamist militants. Benkirane broke with the banned Muslim Youths in 1980; he then took small steps to reassure the security apparatus in exchange for help integrating loose Islamist groups into the legal associations.

In the 1990s, two developments aided Benkirane's project. First, a civil war consumed neighboring Algeria after the military canceled elections that Islamists were poised to sweep in 1992. Second, a radical new clerical movement was highly critical of Morocco's participation with U.S. forces in the 1990–91 Gulf War to liberate Kuwait after Iraq's invasion.

In 1992, Benkirane was allowed to establish Reform and Renewal (al Islah wa Tajdid), a group that conspicuously dropped the name of Islam even though it was an Islamic association. It changed its name to the Movement of Unity and Reform (Harakat al Tawhid wal Islah, or MUR) in 1996, after three regional groups joined in. The new movement provided the social and religious backbone of the future political party.

CO-OPTATION

The PJD, officially formed in 1998, was the product of a gradual and lengthy process of negotiations among fragmented Islamic groups and compromises with authorities. Some of those groups sought to influence state policies from within; others worked to reform society from below. But both accepted the principle of working within the confines of a pluralist autocracy.

The division of labor helps to explain why the PJD's pragmatism—or domestication—did not translate into the ideological transformation expected from a party that claims "Muslim democracy" as a guiding political philosophy. The PJD remains dependent on the socially conservative MUR for leadership, recruitment, and popular support. The majority of the PJD's General Secretariat holds leadership positions in MUR, a factor that is pivotal to election mobilization. So MUR's ideological orientation and spheres of influence are powerful, even though the PJD and MUR are organizationally distinct.

Unlike the PJD, the MUR has to respond to poor, urban, and middle-class constituencies that link endemic state corruption and social injustice to moral decay. Beyond general morality, however, MUR lacks a coherent ideology. Its positions are a blend of pragmatism on local issues, the social activism of Egypt's Muslim Brotherhood, and the reformist spirit of Muslim modernists. This ideological triad is reflected in the MUR's founding text, *al Mithaq*, which is written in accessible language with Koranic quotes and in a short political pamphlet with vague references to democracy and freedom of faith.

Yet the differences between the PJD and the MUR should not be exaggerated; both accept the monarchy's religious attributes and central political role. As of 1997, the PJD and the MUR ran in electoral contests as a single movement.

With the blessing of Moroccan authorities, the MUR was allowed to contest its first elections in 1997 under the name of an already existing party—a virtually empty, inactive political shell called the Popular Democratic and Constitutional Movement. The Islamists changed the party's name to the PJD in 1998. Since then, the PJD has participated in every local and national election, winning progressively more seats in the parliament and on major urban municipal councils.

The party strategy showed self-restraint by initially running fewer candidates to avoid the "Algerian syndrome," where Islamists did so well in the 1991 and 1992 elections that the Algerian military canceled the democratic transition. The PJD's main objective was twofold: First, it wanted to prove that Moroccan Islamists were not a threat to the political system. Second, it sought to prove that Islamists could also be loyal public servants who understood social policies, economic constraints, and the gradual legislative process.

THE MORALIST PHASE

The PJD's evolution can be divided into two distinct phases: the moralist phase from 1997 to 2003 and the legislative phase from 2004 to 2012. These phases reflect changing dynamics within the parliament, the government, the general public, and other political parties, as well as the changing dynamics between the party and its social wing, the MUR.

During the first phase, the PJD contested two major legislative elections in 1997 and 2002. In the 1997 poll, the party ran only 140 candidates, although it could have competed in all of the 325 contested districts. It won fourteen seats in its first attempt at parliamentary politics.

The outcome was significant on three counts: First, the electoral process was not free or transparent and did not reflect the PJD's real political weight at the time. Second, the party opted for self-restraint, which meant not winning too many seats. And third, the PJD took seats from older and more experienced parties, including the socialist party, with well-established networks in major cities such as Casablanca.

In the more transparent 2002 elections, the PJD won forty-two seats even though it again voluntarily restricted its participation. The Ministry of the Interior also took away another dozen seats from the PJD for dubious reasons. Again, the Islamists demonstrated that they could not only compete with well-established non-Islamic parties but could also defeat them in major urban centers. The PJD strategy was to present new, young, and educated candidates with moral values.

In the end, however, the PJD's actual performance once in parliament between 1997 and 2002 was unimpressive. The PJD was crippled by an eagerness to show political moderation and compliance, for which it compensated by showcasing commitment to strict moral values. Instead of taking on the government over substantive political problems or key social and economic policies, PJD deputies focused on restricting the sale of alcohol, "satanic" music, foreign movies, sexual conduct, or inappropriate public behavior. The party's official newspaper, *Attajdid*, also opened its columns to well-known Salafi figures who issued highly controversial fatwas.

THE LEGISLATIVE PHASE

Moroccan politics was transformed in May 2003, when five suicide bombers struck tourist sites and Jewish sites in Casablanca. Scores of people were killed or injured. A radical Islamist group was responsible, but the attacks put the PJD and its social movement, the MUR, on the defensive. Their leaders were blocked from taking part in mass demonstrations led by civil society, other political parties, and trade unions. The palace, other political players, and some public sector officials implied that the PJD carried a moral responsibility for the attacks. Some even called for the party to be dissolved, while parliament—with the PJD's endorsement—passed a new law banning political parties that were based on religious, linguistic, or ethnic grounds.

For the PJD, emphasis on social conservatism and moral issues—both often associated with radical causes—was no longer tenable after the 2003 terrorist attacks. The bombings also increased tensions between the party and its movement, although the more pragmatic politicians ultimately gained the upper hand. As a result, the PJD's parliamentary activities became a priority, but not without a political cost.

The first major test of the PJD's energized political agenda was the vote in 2003 on a controversial antiterrorism bill. The bill restricted freedom of expression and civil rights and gave the government sweeping powers to arrest and prosecute any person involved in activities interpreted as supporting terrorism. Although reluctant, PJD deputies voted collectively for the bill. Another test was the passage of a highly controversial bill in support of women's rights. In 2005, the PJD endorsed a new family code, or *Mudawana*, that gave women more legal rights in matters of marriage, divorce, and child custody.

Yet the PJD's evolution was not simply maneuvering to survive a hostile environment. PJD representatives also brought new insight into two important pivotal debates: the conflict between national security and civil liberties, and the challenge of reconciling modern women's rights with Islamic traditions.

In televised parliamentary debates, the PJD blasted the official response to terrorism as a means of silencing independent or opposition voices. On family law, PJD deputies justified their votes to reform laws on three grounds: First, the legislation was approved by religious leaders. Second, the law would help women and families. And third, the law was the product of a democratic process that involved broad consultations with civil society, women's groups, and political parties.

The PJD parliamentary bloc also became diligent about the legislative process, even circulating its attendance list at a body notorious for absenteeism. It provided its deputies with specialized staff members to help draft and propose bills and technical expertise on policy issues. It also submitted the largest number of oral and written questions to the government.

But the shift from a moralist agenda to legislative activism did not pay off. The PJD was still distrusted by the regime's hardliners. It was isolated from both governing and opposition parties. And it was circumscribed by rules imposed from the palace. In the end, it had no impact on government policy and passed no bills of its own.

The party's underperformance in the 2007 legislative elections further exposed the limits of the PJD's strategy and renewed old tensions between the party and its restless social movement, the MUR. The PJD fielded candidates in ninety-four out of ninety-five contested districts for the vote. Contrary to several poll findings and independent political analyses, however, the party added only four seats—for a total of forty-six seats.

The PJD's poor showing in 2007 had more to do with low voter turnout than with electoral violations and administrative interference (which were still serious problems). Voter turnout plummeted from 58 percent in 1997 to 51 percent in 2002 and then to 37 percent in 2007, according to the government. And the figures did not reflect the millions of unregistered voters (mainly young city dwellers) and the historically high rate of voided votes (30 percent of ballots in some urban centers).

Just fifteen years after it was founded, the PJD was becoming part of the discredited establishment that it had joined to reform from within. On the eve of the Arab Spring in 2011, the party was struggling to define its role, mission, and strategy. But the popular revolts in Tunisia, Egypt, Yemen, and Libya gave the PJD a new political opportunity. The regime began to use the PJD to stave off the winds of political change that might blow from other parts of the Arab world.

JUSTICE AND CHARITY

The PJD's main Islamist competitor is Justice and Charity, or al Adl wal Ihssan. The movement's main objective is the establishment of a just society with equal distribution of resources and an accountable government that enforces Islamic law. Beyond utopian references to a state and society modeled after the Prophet Mohammed's era, the movement does not offer clear and practical alternatives. But it does not promote violence and seemed to be undergoing an ideological transformation after the Arab Spring. For the first time, the movement began to float ideas of a civic state, popular sovereignty, and minority rights.

Because of Justice and Charity's dogmatic positions, the government has not allowed the movement to integrate into politics as a formal party. Justice and Charity's activities remain illegal but not exactly clandestine. The movement recruits students at universities, among primary and secondary school instructors, at mosques in marginal urban districts, and in poor neighborhoods.

Despite preaching peaceful change through education and social work, the movement's leaders and followers continue to face severe repression. After the 2003 bombings, they were targeted during public rallies held to propagate their cause. They were again targeted in 2011, after participating in mass demonstrations sponsored by the February 20 movement.

The mysticism of Yassin—a member of the Zaouia al Boutchichiya Order—might seem ideologically at odds with the movement's positions, which appear more militant than traditionally spiritual Sufi orders. But in Morocco's historical context, mystical figures have often risen to advise or even challenge sultans who abused power or neglected governing responsibilities.

Hence, Yassin's first public appearance in 1974 was an audacious 114-page letter titled "Islam or the Flood" that was addressed to King Hassan II. Presented in the traditional "Mirror for Princes" writing, the public letter exhorted the king to redeem himself if he wanted to save his throne, by following the model of the Prophet's companions. The letter was sent after two abortive military coups and attempts on the life of the king (in 1971 and 1972). Yassin invited the sovereign to stop ruling like a despot, amassing wealth, oppressing people, and disregarding Islamic teachings. The message was clear: if the sovereign did not heed the advice and reform, he would face the wrath of God and the people (what Yassin called *qiyyama*, or revolution).

The government responded by holding Yassin without trial in a psychiatric hospital for more than three years. Since his release, the cleric has repeatedly admonished King Hassan II and then his son Mohammed VI—only to again be detained, sentenced to prison, and put under virtual house arrest.

Justice and Charity's poorly articulated ideology is reflected mainly in the writings of a single charismatic figure, but the movement's goal is for radical, even republican, change in Morocco. Yet in 2011, Justice and Charity was struggling to define its role. Its refusal either to participate in the political process or to try to overthrow the regime through mass demonstrations raised questions about its long-term effectiveness. It suspended participation in the February 20 activities and criticized the PJD in an open letter for agreeing to lead a government heavily constrained by the palace. This ambiguity is unlikely to be resolved without a leadership change or a split within the movement.

THE FUTURE

On paper, the 2011 elections gave the Justice and Development Party significant power to help chart the next five years. It won 107 seats out of 395 seats in the Chamber of Deputies. It controlled eleven of thirty-one cabinet posts. Its victory seemed particularly decisive given Morocco's fragmented political landscape and system of proportional representation, in which no one party or even two parties can claim a majority.

Yet it is hard to be optimistic about the PJD's political future. Although the constitution was amended to give the prime minister more powers, the king can still veto, formally or informally, any decisions or policies he does not like. The political environment remains depressed, with no specific benchmarks or timetable from the new government to get out of the crisis. The PJD-led government appears unable to defuse the explosive social climate or pay for promised social services. It has not offered direction on how to energize the economy given the global economic crisis. Its opening statement was little more than a list of good intentions.

On key issues such as democracy, women's rights, religious freedom, and ethnic groups, the PJD's statements have remained inconsistent and often contradictory. The PJD has dropped the label "Islamist" and embraced the principles of modern democracy, but the party is drastically different from the Turkish party of the same name, which it claims to emulate. Its documents sometimes vary from what its members of parliament actually say. And leaders may qualify and correct each other when there has been a public outcry about particular statements. Benkirane's unprepared and corrosive comments about women, the Amazigh minority, and homosexuals produced particular scorn from many civil society groups.

For the majority of Moroccans, dissatisfaction with the electoral process has been reflected in the historically low rates of voter participation and disproportionately high rates of voided votes. The monarchy seemed to respond quickly to the demands of the February 20 movement, fearing the heat of the Arab Spring. But the constitutional amendments announced in March 2011 and legislative elections in November 2011 were widely perceived as futile maneuvers to preempt a local Arab Spring.

The PJD's influence has so far been so limited that the party faces the real prospect of being discredited by the time it faces another election in 2016. One scenario suggests that the PJD could face the same fate as the discredited socialists did in 2000, when their program to reform the monarchy from within collapsed.

Abdeslam Maghraoui is associate professor of political science at Duke University and member of the Duke Islamic Studies Center. He is author of Liberalism without Democracy *(2006) and a series of papers on the challenge of democratization in the Maghreb. He studies comparative politics of the Middle East and North Africa with a focus on the interplay between culture and politics.*

CHAPTER 11

Jordan: The Quiescent Opposition

Jillian Schwedler

Since the late 1980s, the Islamic Action Front in Jordan has been the leading opposition movement, often boldly challenging the monarchy's domestic and foreign policies. It boycotted the 2010 parliamentary elections and called for a constitutional monarchy led by an elected parliament. In 2011, the Front called for abrogation of the peace treaty signed with Israel in 1994 and the permanent closing of the Israeli embassy in Amman. The moves were particularly provocative in the context of Arab uprisings elsewhere.

Yet the Front was relatively quiescent during the 2011 protests in Jordan demanding reforms. The group, which was formed in 1992 and has been the main Islamist party in elections ever since, describes itself as the "loyal opposition" party. The protests it organized rarely exceeded 1,000 people. And the demonstrations always refrained from calling for an overthrow of the regime. The Front focused instead on the resignation of the prime minister or on specific policies.

The Islamic Action Front's willingness to work within the system is not surprising given the long association between the monarchy and the Muslim Brotherhood, from which the Islamist group was born and to which it still has umbilical ties. The Brotherhood has had a symbiotic relationship with the Hashemite monarchy, particularly during the 1950s and 1960s when Jordanian and Palestinian leftist and militant groups threatened the regime.

In 1989, when Jordan held its first election since the 1967 war, most of the Islamist candidates were affiliated with the Brotherhood, which won the largest bloc in parliament. Over the decades, both the Brotherhood and the Front have repeatedly expressed loyalty to the regime.

Unlike many Islamist parties, the Front has no militant wing. It supports Hamas and opposes Jordan's peace treaty with Israel, but within Jordan it has remained loyal to the regime. Jordan does have an emerging militant Islamist movement. The Salafi trend was largely inspired by Abu Musab al Zarqawi—the Jordanian head of al Qaeda in Iraq, who was assassinated in 2006. Jordan also has a decades-old quiescent Salafi trend.

But the Front has remained distinct from both the Salafists and al Qaeda. Ideologically, it does not share the extremist views of Salafi movements. The

Front has an established record of working within democratic institutions and, indeed, has well-functioning democratic practices within the party itself. It also has a record of cross-ideological cooperation with groups such as leftists and liberals, particularly around issues of political freedoms, a free press, and human rights. However, the Front has conservative positions on women, encouraging only limited political participation and unsuccessfully proposing gender segregation in 1990.

THE BEGINNING

The Islamic Action Front was created as an umbrella Islamist party, but it has always been dominated by the Muslim Brotherhood. The roots of both date back to 1945, when a group of Jordanian merchants who supported a religious jihad against the Zionists in Palestine founded a branch of the Muslim Brotherhood in Jordan.

King Abdullah I supported the Brotherhood and more generally used the Islamists to buttress his regime's own limited support base. In its early days, the Hashemite monarchy relied on several conservative actors, including tribal leaders, minorities, and religious groups. The Muslim Brotherhood emerged as the most powerful of the latter. On November 19, 1945, the king inaugurated the Muslim Brotherhood office in Amman and formally welcomed the group as a religious charitable society. The Brotherhood has been a prominent actor on Jordan's social and political scene ever since. The monarchy also saw the Islamist movement as a counterweight to the growing strength of the National Socialist Party, the other main political alternative.

After 1948, the Brotherhood played a pivotal role in supporting the regime as waves of Palestinian refugees—many of whom embraced leftist and Arab nationalist ideologies—introduced a more politically active constituency into Jordanian politics. It attracted many Palestinians into its ranks through both social support and a tough political message. The Brotherhood declared an unwavering anti-Zionist position and called for Muslim unity against foreign intervention in the Middle East.

In terms of ideology, the Brotherhood's first program gave primary priority to full implementation of Sharia in all spheres of life—political, social, and economic. The Brotherhood has always justified working with the Hashemite regime, however, and has not sought to establish a caliphate or called for an end to the monarchy. The group originally listed its second priority as the full liberation of all of Muslim Palestine. But this goal has not appeared as a priority in its rhetoric since the 1960s, and it did not support Palestinian militants who challenged the regime in the 1960s and early 1970s.

Since at least the 1950s, the Brotherhood leadership has consisted primarily of professionals. Although the Brotherhood has consistently opposed Western imperialism in the Muslim world, Jordan's mainstream Islamists have never been a militant or radical movement. They have sought to promote their social reform program within the regime-defined constraints, although they have frequently pushed to have those constraints loosened.

By 2012, the Brotherhood's support base remained largely unchanged. The movement's social services have won support in poor areas. It has also been popular among Palestinians—particularly refugees residing in bleak camps. Most of Jordan was and remains socially conservative, so the messages of the Muslim Brotherhood and the Islamic Action Front have found a ready audience.

THE EVOLUTION

The first phase of Islamic political activism stretched from independence in 1946 through reforms in 1989. Under the young King Hussein, Jordan had a vibrant political environment. In the mid-1950s, he allowed a range of new and weak political parties to function in an experiment with multiparty politics until leftist and nationalist forces began to challenge the monarchy.

In 1957, however, the regime survived an attempted military coup by Nasserists and leftist officers. The king responded by introducing martial law and outlawing all political parties. The regime continued to hold regular elections, although candidates were all required to run as independents. Parliament met regularly until the 1967 war led to a suspension of the assembly. It did not meet again until 1984.

During this period, the Muslim Brotherhood still functioned as a legal social organization even though all other nonstate groups were banned. In the late 1950s and 1960s, members of Jordan's socialist and communist parties were subject to repression and imprisonment for their support of the Arab nationalist movement. But the king gave the Brotherhood considerable latitude in pursuing its conservative social reform agenda. In turn, the movement's leaders defended the regime's actions.

The events surrounding Black September in the 1970s illustrated the strong ties between the regime and the Brotherhood. Despite the movement's support of an exclusively Arab Palestine, Brotherhood leaders did not back Palestinian militants in their confrontations with the monarchy over their bases in the East Bank. The decision did cause discord within Brotherhood ranks, but those who favored strong ties with the regime prevailed.

Over the decades, the monarchy has even tapped prominent Brotherhood members—including its founding secretary-general—for formal government positions. Other members have also held cabinet posts or high office, including positions in the Ministry of Education and the Ministry of Religious Affairs and Endowments. One of King Hussein's top goals—and successes—was eliminating illiteracy. In 1961, the illiteracy rate was 67.6 percent. By 1995, it had plummeted to 14.3 percent. Tapping Brotherhood members for illiteracy projects indicated the close relationship between the regime and the movement.

At the same time, the monarchy never fully co-opted the Brotherhood. The movement was granted space to pursue its agenda as long as those activities did not challenge the regime's sovereignty. Members were occasionally arrested and imprisoned for criticizing government practices. In the late 1950s, the group challenged the regime for its ongoing relations with Britain—particularly Britain's role in advising the Jordanian regime on military and security issues. At the same time, the Brotherhood supported King Hussein's imposition of martial law to contain leftist radicalism.

THE ISLAMIC ACTION FRONT'S CREATION

Jordan reconvened its parliament in 1984 with by-elections to fill vacant seats from the 1967 assembly. But phase two really began in 1989, with the first full election for a new assembly, held in response to protests over economic grievances that began in the south and spread throughout the kingdom. Brotherhood members participated in the protests but did not organize them. Nor was the protest characterized by Islamist rhetoric.

But the Islamists profited from the opposition. In the 1989 elections, Islamist candidates won the largest bloc, with thirty-four of eighty seats in parliament. In light of their electoral success, Islamists were given five cabinet positions. They then generated considerable outrage by trying to introduce limited gender segregation and ban alcohol. The king dismissed the controversial cabinet within six months of the election. Since then, only Islamists who have formally left the Brotherhood have won cabinet positions.

In the 1989 poll, the Brotherhood had a strong advantage over other political groups. It had held a license to operate as a social organization since 1957, whereas political parties had been outlawed. The Brotherhood also had a well-established network of regional offices.

Since its creation, the Brotherhood has recruited around family or kinship cells, or *usrah*. Its networks have been tightened through intermarriage of followers and close personal connections. The group also runs a well-established network of Islamic charitable institutions, clinics, mosques, and schools. In 1989, the Brotherhood tapped these small, localized groups to mobilize support for its candidates and the creation of a formal political party.

After the 1989 elections, the monarchy lifted martial law and expanded political freedoms. Political parties were legalized in late 1992. But the Brotherhood opted not to refashion itself into a political party—a reaction, in part, to a new law forbidding parties with ties to political groups outside of Jordan. The leadership decided that the Brotherhood should retain its character as a charitable social organization focused primarily on education, health care, and the spread of Islamic values.

The Islamic Action Front was formed in September 1992 by 353 Jordanian Islamists, including 11 women. This committee originally conceptualized the Front as an umbrella party for Islamists from all trends, but independents soon complained of Brotherhood dominance. A year after its creation, the Front was widely recognized as the de facto political party of the Muslim Brotherhood, even as the organizations remain legally separate.

The new party included democratic mechanisms for representation and accountability. It meets annually and elects a 120-person consultative council that serves four-year terms. The council sets party policy and elects the council chairperson, the party secretary-general, and the members of the executive bureau to two-year terms. Reflecting philosophical ties, the Front's offices are often physically close to Brotherhood facilities, sometimes sharing the same spaces.

INFLUENCE EBBS

The third phase of Islamist activism stretched from 1993 through the ascent of King Abdullah II in 1999 after King Hussein's death. The Front participated in the 1993 elections but fared considerably poorer after redistricting and substantive changes in election laws. The system used in 1989 allowed each voter to cast as many ballots as there were seats from that constituency. Political groups, including the Brotherhood, benefited from this system because voters could cast ballots for local elites as well as ideological groups. In the 1989 assembly, Islamists controlled 40 percent of the seats, and leftists controlled another 16 percent, giving the opposition a majority.

In the 1993 contest, however, each voter could cast only one ballot. The new law dramatically reduced the Front's representation in parliament. The Islamist bloc won thirty-four seats in 1989, but only twenty-two seats in 1993. (Leftist parties also saw their share reduced, from thirteen to seven seats.)

The regime needed the new law not only because a large opposition bloc made it nervous, but also because the regime hoped to conclude a peace treaty with Israel, so it needed a compliant assembly to approve the treaty. The regime achieved that goal by changing the election law. The treaty with Israel was signed in 1994 and soon thereafter was ratified by parliament.

Although the Front had long-standing tensions with leftist groups, their mutual frustration with the monarchy after the 1993 election led to cooperation on issues of common interest. The new joint opposition bloc met regularly, held joint press conferences, and co-organized protests. The former rivals continued to be divided over women's status. But the bloc stood together in boycotting the 1997 parliamentary elections. The bloc's primary grievances were the election law and changes to press and publications laws.

SIDELINED

After King Abdullah II took the throne in 1999, the Front felt increasingly sidelined. The party lost all representation in parliament as a result of the 1997 boycott. Even more important, the decades-old relationship between the Muslim Brotherhood and King Hussein had come to an end. King Abdullah II showed no interest in courting even moderate Islamists, and he did not have the personal relationships with the party's leaders that his father had enjoyed.

The Front felt even further isolated when elections due to be held in 2001 were postponed, partly in response to waves of protests. Demonstrations first erupted in Jordan following the second Palestinian intifada in September 2000 and again in spring 2002, after the Israeli invasion of several West Bank towns, including Nablus and Jenin. Both the Front and the Brotherhood joined the protests but did not organize them.

The Islamists became increasingly worried about being permanently marginalized. In 2001, al Qaeda's 9/11 attacks pushed concern about Islamists onto the center stage globally, and groups such as the Front had to go on the defensive. Its leaders were frustrated that a long history of working within the political system and eschewing violence were forgotten. They struggled to demonstrate that they remained a "loyal opposition" and even organized events in solidarity with Americans immediately after the attacks in New York and Washington. But King Abdullah II still held the Front at arm's length. He introduced economic reforms but simultaneously retreated from many of the political advances introduced during his father's rule in the early 1990s.

In 2003, the Front decided to run again for parliament. It won seventeen seats, including a seat for its first female candidate, who won one of six new quota seats for women. But Jordan's parliament had lost significant power over the years, and by 2007 the party was divided over whether to contest the elections. In the end, it did offer candidates.

In the 2007 vote, which was widely criticized for manipulation by the regime, the Front won only 6 of 110 parliamentary seats. The party subsequently divided, with a hawkish wing opposed to participating in elections. After several internal debates, it decided to boycott the 2010 elections. One female member defied the boycott and won one of the twelve quota seats for women. Immediately after the election, the Front called for a move toward a constitutional monarchy.

In 2011, the Arab uprisings swept the region, including protests almost weekly in parts of Jordan. But protests in the kingdom never reached the scale of protests elsewhere, nor did protesters demand the overthrow of the regime. The Front organized a number of protests in downtown Amman, but participation seldom exceeded 1,000 demonstrators.

KEY POSITIONS

Democracy

The Front has consistently promoted democracy and political freedoms. It has cooperated with leftist and liberal parties, particularly on those issues. Internally, the party also practices democratic politics, with various groups of hawks and doves rotating in and out of the party's executive offices.

Women's Rights

The Front has had women elected to its consultative council, the highest decision-making body. Although it has consistently encouraged women to vote in national and municipal elections, it has fielded female candidates for national elections only since the introduction of the women's quota in 2003. Party officials contend that they support women's full political rights, but they have consistently opposed legislation to increase the rights of women in a divorce and the rights of women's children to citizenship. The party also opposed efforts to change laws pertaining to honor crimes, although officials individually express their opposition to the practice.

Relations with Other Parties

The Front has cooperated with leftist and liberal parties since 1993 in both official and unofficial capacities. Cooperation has been limited to issues of political reform and does not involve issues of social reform—particularly issues concerning women's rights.

Relations with Palestinians

The Front leadership includes Jordanian citizens of both Palestinian and East Bank origin. It is not the only party that advocates for Palestinians, but it is easily the most popular party among them.

United States

The Front is critical of U.S. intervention in the region and has organized many protest events against the United States for its support of Israel and its invasion of Iraq. The party refuses to meet in an official capacity with U.S. officials, although it welcomes American researchers. In private, Front officials are divided over whether the group should engage with the United States.

Israel/Palestine

The Front has held a consistent position against Jordan's peace treaty with Israel, as summarized in its 2003 election platform: "In all cases, working to liberate Palestine is a central concern in relations to all Muslims. No entity has the right to concede any part of Palestine or give legitimacy to the occupation on any part of its holy land. Our struggle with the Jews is creedal and civilizational. It cannot be ended by a peace treaty. It is a struggle over existence, not borders."

OTHER ISLAMISTS

The Muslim Brotherhood and Islamic Action Front dominate Islamist politics in Jordan, but there are other Islamist voices. The Brotherhood has complex relations with many of these groups.

HAMAS AND THE PALESTINIAN MUSLIM BROTHERHOOD

Jordan's Brotherhood has long had close links to Hamas, a militant movement that emerged in Gaza out of the Palestinian branch of the Muslim Brotherhood in 1987. From 1948 to 1967, when Jordan controlled the West Bank, the Palestinian Brotherhood was organizationally connected to the Jordanian Brotherhood. They shared office space and members, although the Palestinian branch had a separate overseer.

When Jordan lost control of the West Bank in 1967, the Palestinian Brotherhood began closer cooperation with the movement's Gaza branch. The creation of Hamas in 1987—with an armed wing—marked a significant departure from the Muslim Brotherhood's longtime strategy of reform-based engagement. Organizationally, however, the Palestinian Muslim Brotherhood (now referred to only as Hamas) remains attached to the Jordanian Muslim Brotherhood, and Hamas offices still exist within the Muslim Brotherhood directorate in Amman. However, as a general rule the Jordanian Muslim Brotherhood has consistently put its own survival and relations with the monarchy ahead of Palestinian liberation, most notably in supporting the regime during the 1970 events of Black September.

The Islamic Center Party (Hizb al Wasat al Islami)

The Islamic Center Party emerged in 2003 with liberal commitments to pluralism, equality, and human rights. The founders included several independent Islamists who were originally members of the Front but who resigned because of the Brotherhood's domination of the party. The Islamic Center Party is very small and unproven on the political scene.

The Liberation Party (Hizb al Tahrir)

At the other end of the ideological spectrum, the Liberation Party was founded in Jerusalem in 1952, when the city was under Jordanian control. Jordan denied the Liberation Party's application to form a legal political party because the party failed to recognize the Jordanian constitution and sought to replace the monarchy with an Islamic state. Brotherhood leaders claim that this party plotted several assassination attempts against King Hussein and sought to seize power in 1962. Others contend that the party has never advocated violence against the monarchy, and scholars have noted that no records of such activities exist. Party leaders tried again to register as a legal party in 1992 but were denied registration.

Salafi Groups

Various Islamist networks and groups function throughout the kingdom, but they have seldom played pivotal political roles. A Salafi movement emerged in the 1970s when Jordanians exposed to Salafi ideas while studying in Egypt, Lebanon, and Syria returned to the kingdom.

The movement has always had rival reformist and jihadi trends. The jihadist faction gained strength in 1989 with the return of fighters from Afghanistan who advocated violence to achieve an Islamic society. The question of *takfir*—the practice of declaring someone a *kafir*, or infidel, thus providing justification for violence—is the central dispute among Jordan's Salafists. Prominent Salafi leaders are located in Zarqa and Irbid, and their circles seem to gain members through the defection of Islamists from the Muslim Brotherhood and the Islamic Missionary Society.

Information about support for Osama bin Laden or al Qaeda is thin; by most counts, bin Laden had no following prior to the 9/11 attacks even among Salafi circles. Interest in extremist tactics increased with the prominence of Abu Musab al Zarqawi, a native of the conservative town of Zarqa, northwest of Amman. His followers carried out the deadly 2005 bombings in three Amman hotels. Yet Jordan's jihadists seem to have gained only a modest following, although enough that the Front and other mainstream Islamists expressed concern about losing their hawkish constituency to the militants. During the Arab uprisings in 2011, Salafi jihadists demonstrated on several occasions to demand release of imprisoned members, once bringing knives and clubs and clashing with the riot police.

Islamic Missionary Society (Jamaat Tabligh)

The Islamic Missionary Society rejects direct involvement in political activities but seeks adherence to strict Islamic practices. The society spreads its vision through education—notably through free literacy classes and discussion groups organized in poorer neighborhoods.

THE FUTURE

The Front shows no signs of deviating from its long history as Jordan's loyal opposition. Its reluctance to generate mass protests in 2011 underlined its commitment to working within the system to implement political reforms. With a small but growing jihadi trend in Jordan, the Front has sought to appeal to the regime as being a stabilizer that can counter extremism while advancing a conservative Islamic social agenda.

But the party's commitment to democratic political reform has significant limits, most notably its serious reluctance to advance gender equality. In the coming years, the Front is likely to continue along this path: joining the chorus for political liberalization but resisting the cosmopolitan and liberal social image that the monarchy has worked hard to present to the outside world.

Jillian Schwedler is associate professor of political science at the University of Massachusetts, Amherst. She is the author of Faith in Moderation: Islamist Parties in Jordan and Yemen *(2006) and coeditor of* Policing and Prisons in the Middle East *(2010). Her website is http://polsci.umass.edu/profiles/schwedler_jillian.*

CHAPTER 12

Lebanon: The Shiite Dimension

Nicholas Blanford

Lebanon's main Islamist party has undergone one of the most profound transformations across the Muslim world over the past three decades. Once associated with suicide bombings and hostage taking, the party has steadily evolved from an underground movement in 1982 to the leading influence inside the Lebanese government by 2012.

Hezbollah, or the Party of God, still has two faces, however. It was powerful enough at home to force the resignation of Prime Minister Saad Hariri in 2011 simply by pulling out of Lebanon's coalition government. But Hezbollah also remained the most powerful regional militia, using its vast arsenal to fight Israel for thirty-four days in 2006. The conflict was Israel's longest Middle East war. Across the region, Hezbollah chief Sheikh Hassan Nasrallah also regularly tops popularity polls. The movement, created under Iran's auspices and aid after Israel's 1982 invasion, reflects the dynamic Shiite dimension of Islamist politics in the Arab world.

Hezbollah was inspired by the teachings of Iranian revolutionary leader Ayatollah Ruhollah Khomeini. It subscribes to a doctrine known as the *velayat-e faqih*—or, in Arabic, the *wali al-faqih*—Khomeini's theory of Islamic governance, which bestows guardianship of government to a senior religious scholar. Iran remains Hezbollah's chief ideological, financial, and military supporter. Syria is also a close ally.

Hezbollah's core ideological goals are resisting Israel, establishing an Islamic state in Lebanon, and offering obedience to Iran's supreme leader. But Hezbollah has developed a keen sense of realpolitik that has helped shape its political agenda and allowed it to sidestep challenges to its armed status. It long ago accepted, for example, that an Islamic state is not appropriate for Lebanon, and it has considered alternative systems of government.

Hezbollah has deepened its involvement in Lebanese politics over the years, but it does so with some hesitation and usually only in response to changed situations or threats to its core interests. Ideally, the party would prefer to avoid the pitfalls of Lebanon's political quagmire, believing that it complicates the more pressing goal of confronting Israel.

"We have never sought to be in government ministries," Nasrallah said after the collapse of the Saad Hariri government in 2011. "All we have been saying to successive governments—and we still say it today—is the following:

Brothers, we are a resistance movement.... We do not seek to run the government. Our hearts and minds are elsewhere. When people go to sleep, we conduct [military] training and prepare ourselves."

Hezbollah has never been stronger militarily and politically, but the challenges facing the movement have also never been greater. They range from rising domestic discontent over Hezbollah's refusal to abandon its weapons to the Syrian uprising, which threatens to unseat the regime of President Bashar al Assad and alter the geostrategic balance in the Middle East.

Over three decades, its deepening political engagement has also transformed Hezbollah into the main representative of Lebanon's Shiites, the largest of the country's seventeen recognized sects. In turn, the movement now needs continued support of the community to ensure its own survival. Yet the interests of its constituents do not always correspond to the agenda of Iran's leaders, to whom Hezbollah is ideologically beholden. Balancing these rival obligations is a paradox that Hezbollah is finding ever more difficult to reconcile.

THE BEGINNING

Hezbollah emerged in the wake of Israel's 1982 invasion of Lebanon, but its genesis lay in the Shiite religious seminaries of Najaf in southern Iraq. In the 1960s and 1970s, Lebanese clerical students were influenced by leading Shiite ideologues such as Mohammed Baqir al Sadr and Ruhollah Khomeini. Sadr, a founder of the Party of the Islamic Call, or Hizb al Dawa al Islamiyya, promoted Islamic values as a counterweight to secularism and the leftist ideologies then attracting the Arab young. Khomeini achieved prominence with his doctrine of *velayat-e faqih*.

After Iraqi President Saddam Hussein's crackdown on the Shiite clerical establishment in the late 1970s, Lebanese students and teachers were forced to return home. Some then began to preach the ideas of Khomeini and Sadr to a domestic audience.

By the end of the 1970s, three developments helped create fertile ground for the eventual emergence of Hezbollah. One factor was the creation of Amal, the first strong Shiite movement. Amal's founder was Sayyed Musa Sadr, a charismatic Iranian-born cleric who tapped into rising anger among Shiites over their repression by other Lebanese sects, particularly Christians and Sunni Muslims. But in 1978, Sadr vanished during a trip to Libya. After his disappearance, Amal drifted in a more secular direction under new leadership, to the dismay of the movement's Islamists.

The second event was Israel's first invasion of Lebanon in 1978 in a bid to expel the Palestine Liberation Organization (PLO). Israel installed a security cordon along the border inside Lebanon, which was controlled by an Israeli-backed militia. It was the first experience for many southern Lebanese in living under occupation.

The third crucial event was the Iranian Revolution in 1979, when the first modern theocracy replaced the dynastic rule that had prevailed in Iran for more than 2,500 years. The revolution had an electrifying effect on Lebanese Shiites in general and on the clerical followers of Khomeini in particular. Iranian leaders and Lebanese clerics held lengthy discussions about importing the revolution to Lebanon and building an armed anti-Israel movement. Among the Lebanese clerics were Sheikh Sobhi Tufayli, who later became Hezbollah's first secretary-general, and Sayyed Abbas Musawi, a preacher from the Bekaa Valley village of Nabi Sheet.

The idea was delayed by an Iranian power struggle and the beginning of the eight-year war between Iran and Iraq in 1980. But then Israel invaded Lebanon in June 1982 to drive the PLO out of Lebanon.

Iran immediately offered assistance, dispatching 5,000 Revolutionary Guards to Syria for deployment in Lebanon. But the main fighting soon ended, and most of the Iranians returned home. Aided by Syria, a smaller contingent of Iranians moved into the northern Bekaa Valley to begin mobilizing and recruiting Shiites into a new anti-Israel force that was the basis of what became Hezbollah.

By 1983, the nascent Hezbollah's influence was seeping from the Bekaa Valley into Beirut's Shiite suburbs and from there further south toward the front line of the Israeli occupation. By 1985, Israel, exhausted by the intensifying resistance campaign, withdrew to a security belt along the Lebanon-Israel border. Hezbollah—along with Amal and secular local resistance groups, which played smaller roles—had more success in pressuring Israel in two years than had the PLO in a decade. Hezbollah won additional support by providing social welfare services to lower-class Shiites.

In 1985, Hezbollah formally declared its existence in its "Open Letter," a manifesto outlining its identity and agenda. The goals included driving Israeli forces from south Lebanon as a precursor to the destruction of the Jewish state and the liberation of Jerusalem. Hezbollah confirmed that it abided by the orders of "a single wise and just command" represented by Ayatollah Khomeini, the "rightly guided imam."

Hezbollah also rejected Lebanon's sectarian political system and instead advocated creation of an Islamic state. At the same time, the party was careful to emphasize that it did not wish to impose Islam as a religion on anyone and that other Lebanese should be free to pick their preferred system of governance.

In formally declaring its existence and goals, Hezbollah emerged from the shadows and demonstrated that it was not a fleeting aberration of the civil war but a force determined to endure.

FIRST PHASE: UNDERGROUND

Hezbollah's evolution falls into four distinct phases. The first was from 1982 to 1990 and coincided with the chaotic 1975–90 civil war, during which the Lebanese state had little control. Lebanon was instead carved into competing fiefdoms dominated by militias and occupying armies. These were Hezbollah's wild days, when it could do as it pleased under Iran's guidance and Syria's watchful eye.

The movement became synonymous with extremist attacks, including two on U.S. embassies in 1983 and 1984. Its deadliest attacks were the simultaneous truck bombings of the U.S. Marine barracks and the nearby French Paratroop headquarters, which killed 241 American servicemen and sixty-eight French soldiers. From 1984, more than 100 foreigners in Lebanon were kidnapped. Hezbollah denied responsibility, although some of its members were later linked with the attacks.

After 1986, Hezbollah dominated the resistance against Israel's occupation in south Lebanon. But the party's growing influence in the south also brought it into conflict with the rival Amal movement. In 1988, the two factions fought the first in a series of bloody internecine battles that over the next two years resulted in thousands of dead and generated an animosity that lingered a quarter-century later.

SECOND PHASE: RUNNING FOR PARLIAMENT

The second phase was from 1991 to 2000, following the end of Lebanon's civil war in 1990. The restoration of state control sparked a debate within Hezbollah over its future course of action. Hardliners, represented by Sheikh Tufayli, argued that Hezbollah should not compromise its ideological agenda regardless of the nation's changed circumstances. Others countered that Hezbollah had to adapt to the new situation to protect its "resistance priority"—the right to confront Israel's continued occupation of the south.

The debate played out over whether Hezbollah should run in the 1992 parliamentary election, the first in twenty years. Joining parliament would strengthen Hezbollah's standing in Lebanon, but it would also flout its 1985 manifesto that rejected a sectarian political system. Pragmatists won after receiving the blessing of Ayatollah Ali Khameini, Iran's supreme leader, to participate in the elections. Hezbollah won eight parliamentary seats.

Hezbollah also went through a leadership change. A few months before the 1992 election, Hezbollah secretary-general Sayyed Abbas Musawi was assassinated in an Israeli helicopter ambush. He was replaced by his protégé, Sayyed Hassan Nasrallah, a thirty-two-year-old cleric.

Under Nasrallah, Hezbollah reorganized, adding new bodies to handle its military, political, and social work. It expanded its social welfare activities nationwide to sustain its popular support within the Shiite community. It also launched a television station, Al-Manar, as the flagship of its propaganda arm, and opened a media relations office. Hezbollah even began a dialogue with other factions and religious representatives, including Christians.

Hezbollah's newfound pragmatism did not represent an ideological softening or a decision to exchange Islamic militancy for a share of Lebanon's political space. Hezbollah was instead adapting to postwar circumstances to safeguard the resistance. Shortly after the 1992 election, Nasrallah explained, "Our participation in the elections and entry into [parliament] do not alter the fact that we are a resistance party."

Hezbollah's resistance efforts actually intensified after 1992. Its hit-and-run guerrilla tactics claimed ever-higher Israeli casualties. In 1993 and 1996, Israel responded with air and artillery blitzes against Lebanon in failed attempts to dent Hezbollah's campaign.

The late 1990s were Hezbollah's "golden years." Hezbollah's military exploits won it admirers across the Arab and Islamic worlds and earned the respect of all Lebanese, even those inclined to view the Shiite party with suspicion. Under growing pressure from Hezbollah, Israel finally ended its occupation in May 2000, the first time that the Jewish state had ceded occupied territory through force of Arab arms.

THIRD PHASE: CONFRONTATION

The third phase was from 2000 to 2005. With Israel's withdrawal, Hezbollah's reputation had never been higher. But its victory was Pyrrhic. A growing number of Lebanese began questioning why Hezbollah needed to keep arms. Hezbollah countered by citing minor territorial disputes and the number of Lebanese still detained in Israeli prisons. It claimed its weapons were a vital part of Lebanon's defense. Hezbollah had to make sure that the Israelis did not come back. Many Lebanese accused Hezbollah of serving an Iranian—rather than Lebanese—agenda. But Hezbollah still enjoyed the political cover afforded by Syria, which continued to endorse the party's armed status.

In February 2005, Rafik Hariri, a former prime minister of Lebanon, was assassinated in a truck bomb explosion. Many Lebanese blamed Damascus, and roughly one-quarter of the country's population took to the streets in protest. Three months later, Syria pulled its troops out of Lebanon, ending three decades of military occupation.

The sudden loss of Syrian cover compelled Hezbollah to take another step deeper into Lebanese politics to defend its "resistance priority." It agreed to an alliance with its longtime Amal rival and with the Free Patriotic Movement, a Christian party led by former General Michel Aoun.

After the 2005 parliamentary election, Hezbollah joined the government for the first time. Yet its participation did not defuse the core issue. Over the following months, Lebanese politics grew increasingly rancorous over Hezbollah's arms. It was the single most divisive national issue.

FOURTH PHASE: WAR AND REBUILDING

The fourth phase ran from 2006 to 2012 and included Hezbollah's biggest military gamble. On July 12, 2006, its militia abducted two Israeli soldiers along the border. The audacious act triggered a devastating monthlong war with Israel. Hezbollah fought the Israeli army to a standstill in south Lebanon and declared a "divine victory"—but at a high cost.

More than 1,100 Lebanese died in the war, which also caused billions of dollars of damage. In the face of intense domestic criticism, Hezbollah walked out of the Lebanese cabinet in November 2006. A month later, Hezbollah tried to force the government to resign by organizing a mass protest in central Beirut. The government stood its ground, but political paralysis gripped Lebanon.

Tensions between Hezbollah and the central government continued. In 2008, the government of Prime Minister Saad Hariri—son of the slain leader—announced it intended to shut down Hezbollah's private telecommunications network. Hezbollah reacted by staging a brief takeover of west Beirut, triggering a week of clashes that left more than 100 people dead and brought the country to the edge of civil war. The crisis ended with the formation of a new government and the long-delayed election of a president, Michel Suleiman.

In 2009, Lebanon faced a new crisis when a United Nations investigation obtained evidence implicating Hezbollah in the assassination of Rafik Hariri four years earlier. Hezbollah denied the allegations and claimed that the Dutch-based tribunal investigating the case was serving the political interests of the United States and Israel.

The Hariri government refused to abandon its support for the tribunal. In January 2011, as the tribunal was preparing to issue its first set of indictments, Hezbollah and its political allies forced a vote of no confidence in the government. The new government was composed of Hezbollah and its allies; it was led by Prime Minister Najib Mikati, a billionaire businessman and political moderate.

By 2012, Hezbollah was the dominant political and military force in Lebanon. Yet as it became more deeply embroiled in rough-and-tumble Lebanese politics, it was also constrained and encumbered by the daily challenges of governing.

KEY POSITIONS

Hezbollah has never abandoned the core ideological pillars listed in its manifesto in 1985: the confrontation against Israel, the observance of the *wilayet al-faqih* leadership doctrine, and the preference to live in an Islamic state.

But the party has adjusted its public discourse and operational behavior over the years to suit the unfolding political and social environment in Lebanon. This survival strategy was evident in the 2009 "Political Document," a long-awaited update to the original "Open Letter." Much of the fiery rhetoric of the earlier manifesto was replaced with nuanced deliberations on a future Lebanese state and the most suitable form of democracy.

Islam and Democracy

In the 1985 "Open Letter," Hezbollah stated, "We do not wish to impose Islam on anybody and we hate to see others impose on us their convictions and their systems. We do not want Islam to rule in Lebanon by force.... But we stress that we are convinced of Islam as a faith, system, thought, and rule, and we urge all to recognize it and resort to its law."

Nearly thirty years later, Hezbollah still wants an Islamic state. Indeed, because Hezbollah is a jihadist Islamist organization, it would be anathema for Hezbollah to renounce the idea of living in a state run under Islamic Sharia law. But its leadership long ago accepted that Lebanon's multisectarian and pluralistic environment is not suited to the establishment of an Islamic state. Instead, Hezbollah has deliberated over acceptable alternatives.

In the 2009 "Political Document," Hezbollah repeated its long-standing rejection of Lebanon's sectarian political system, which it considered "a strong constraint to the achievement of true democracy under which an elected majority may govern and an elected minority may oppose." Until political sectarianism is abolished, Hezbollah argued that "consensual democracy will remain the fundamental basis of governance in Lebanon."

Hezbollah explained:

> The consensual democracy constitutes an appropriate political formula to guarantee true partnership and contributes in opening the doors for everyone to enter the phase of building the reassuring state that makes all its citizens feel that it is founded for their sake.

Women and Personal Freedoms

Hezbollah has a more open attitude toward women's role in society than do many other Islamist organizations. Women play important roles within Hezbollah's social-welfare, media, and administrative departments. In the 2009 "Political Document," Hezbollah said that it sought a state "that works to consolidate the role of women at all levels in the framework of benefiting from their characteristics [and] influence while respecting their status."

Hezbollah does not aggressively interfere in the lifestyles of its Shiite constituents. Certain taboos are observed—for example, Hezbollah bans the sale of alcohol and stamps out drug use in areas under its control—but Hezbollah is generally uninterested in antagonizing its supporters by imposing a strict moral regimen.

Other Religions

Hezbollah recognizes that Lebanon has a diverse religious landscape and has open channels of dialogue with all other sects. Hezbollah has always championed unity between the Shiite and Sunni sects on grounds that resistance against Israel takes precedence over doctrinal differences. Hezbollah counts Sunni Islamists among its allies, despite sporadic Shiite-Sunni tensions. Hezbollah opened a dialogue with the Maronite church for the first time in 1992, and a specially appointed party representantive regularly meets with the religious leaders of various Christian denominations.

The United States and the West

In the 1985 "Open Letter," Hezbollah described the United States as the "first root of vice" and "the reason for all our catastrophes and the source of all malice." That view has not fundamentally changed. The 2009 "Political Document" railed against U.S. global hegemony, accusing it of being the "origin of every aspect of terrorism" and, under the administration of President George W. Bush, "a danger that threatens the whole world in every level and field."

The document stated:

> The unlimited U.S. support for Israel and its cover for the Israeli occupation of Arab lands in addition to the American domination of international institutions and dualism in issuing and implementing international resolutions, the policy of interfering in other states' affairs, militarizing the world and adopting the principle of circulating wars in international conflicts, evoking disorder and turbulence all over the world put the American administration in a position hostile to our nation and peoples and hold it essentially responsible of causing chaos in the international political system.

In the 1980s, Hezbollah listed France, Israel, and the United States as its main enemies. By 2012, however, Hezbollah officials often met with European representatives, and the party's attitude toward Europe was more reproachful than hostile. European policies, Hezbollah said, "fluctuate between incapability and inefficiency on one hand and unjustified subjugation to U.S. policies on the other."

Israel

In the 1985 "Open Letter," Hezbollah explicitly said that Israel "is a usurping enemy that must be fought until the usurped right [i.e., Palestine] is returned to its owners…. Our struggle with usurping Israel emanates from an ideological and historical awareness that this Zionist entity is aggressive in its origins and structure and is built on usurped land and at the expense of the rights of a Muslim people. Therefore, our confrontation of this entity must end with its obliteration from existence."

In the 2009 "Political Document," Hezbollah cited its hostility toward Israel to justify keeping its arms and a military wing:

Israel represents an eternal threat to Lebanon—the state and the entity—and a real danger to the country regarding its historical ambitions in its land and water.

...

The role of the Resistance is a national necessity as long as Israeli threats and ambitions to seize our lands and waters continue, in the absence of the capable strong state and the strategic imbalance between the state and the enemy.

CHIEF ALLIES

Iran is Hezbollah's main financial, military, and logistical supplier, and Iran's supreme leader is the party's ultimate source of authority. Under the late President Hafez al Assad, Syria was Hezbollah's protector and supervisor. Since Assad's son Bashar al Assad took over in 2000, Syria has evolved into an even closer strategic ally. Syria is the vital geostrategic linchpin connecting Iran to Hezbollah, providing strategic depth and a conduit for the transfer of arms.

The Palestinian Hamas movement and Palestinian Islamic Jihad have been allies of Hezbollah since the early 1990s. Both groups have benefited from Iranian financial and material patronage. But Hamas, a Sunni movement, does not share the Shiite ideology of Iran and Hezbollah, making Hamas and Hezbollah uncomfortable bedfellows beyond a shared hostility toward Israel.

Amal and the Free Patriotic Movement are secular Lebanese political entities that have been allied with Hezbollah since 2005 and 2006, respectively. Hezbollah also maintains alliances with smaller pro-Syrian factions and individuals, Islamist groups, and Palestinian groups.

THE FUTURE

In 2012, Hezbollah was arguably the most formidable nonstate military actor in the world. It was also the most powerful political force and dominant influence in the Lebanese government of Prime Minister Najib Mikati.

Yet down the road, Hezbollah also faces grave challenges that derive from its dual and sometimes conflicting roles as both Iran's surrogate and, at the same time, the chief representative of Lebanon's Shiites. Iran has helped transform Hezbollah into a robust and unique military force that serves as a component of Iranian deterrence. Hezbollah is also, however, answerable to the needs and interests of its domestic constituency. The paradox is increasingly hard to reconcile.

Hezbollah's public standing has also declined somewhat since the heady days of the 1990s. Hezbollah's refusal to disarm lies at the heart of Lebanon's festering political divide. Over the years, Hezbollah has been sucked ever deeper into the political mire. It considered its shift into the treacherous and fractious world of Lebanese politics as an unfortunate necessity to better defend its "resistance priority."

The Arab Spring presented another set of difficulties for Hezbollah. It supported uprisings that toppled the leaders of Tunisia, Egypt, and Libya, but it was caught off guard by the nationwide Syrian protests. Repeated declarations of support for the Bashar al Assad regime have eroded the party's popularity, both among Sunnis, who make up the bulk of the Syrian opposition, and in the Arab world, as the regional tensions increase between Shiite Iran and the Sunni Arab states led by Saudi Arabia.

More broadly, the Arab uprisings appear to have dulled the appeal of resistance and jihad for many young Arabs, who for now seem more interested in democracy and new social contracts that provide jobs and opportunity.

Hezbollah will remain a powerful political player on the Lebanese scene for the foreseeable future regardless of developments in Syria. But the challenge for Hezbollah of balancing its ideological and logistical obligations to Iran and its political and social duties to Lebanon's Shiite community is a paradox that will only grow more difficult in the years ahead.

Nicholas Blanford is the Beirut correspondent for The Times of London *and* The Christian Science Monitor. *He is the author of* Killing Mr. Lebanon: The Assassination of Rafik Hariri and Its Impact on the Middle East *(2006) and* Warriors of God: Inside Hezbollah's Thirty-Year Struggle against Israel *(2011).*

CHAPTER 13

Yemen: The Tribal Islamists

Leslie Campbell

In Yemen, tribe is still the core around which political, economic, and social lives are organized. So Islamist politics in the Arab world's poorest country has always blended with tribal influence. Indeed, tribal factors and figureheads often superseded Islam and its sheikhs in the Islah Party or, formally, the Yemeni Congregation for Reform.

Formed in 1990, Islah was an amalgam. It merged three strands of society: tribal forces, which were powerful in rural areas; the Muslim Brotherhood, which was strong in urban areas; and Salafi sheikhs, who ran a network of religious schools. Its political spectrum included traditionalists, pragmatic conservatives, and rigid ultraconservatives. Unlike Islamist parties elsewhere, however, Islah was effectively sponsored by the ruling General People's Congress.

Between 1990 and 1997, the Islamist party was actually part of coalition governments led by President Ali Abdullah Saleh. Between 1997 and 2011, Islah fluctuated between functioning as the largest opposition party and cooperating with the government to influence policy decisions; sometimes the party did both at the same time.

Two major turning points have thrust the Sunni party into a more independent and powerful position. The first was the death of tribal leader Abdullah al Ahmar, one of Yemen's most powerful politicians and a cofounder of Islah. His passing in 2007 diminished the tribal hold over the Islamist party. The second turning point was the 2011 uprising, when Islah emerged as a major power broker in the deal for Saleh's resignation and the transfer of power.

Islah has been a comparatively pragmatic Islamic party. Its political manifesto describes the group as "a popular political organization that seeks reform of all aspects of life on the basis of Islamic principles and teachings." But the manifesto also states that policies must be "centered on the realities and events of their [people's] experiences" as well as "appreciating the network of external and internal factors that influence the running of ... [Yemen's] affairs."

The manifesto, which is less dogmatic than its counterparts in other countries, adds that Islah favors a "gradual approach" to achieving change. In Islah's public rhetoric, pragmatic factors have also increasingly trumped theological considerations. Islah differs from other Islamist parties in the Arab world in its focus on individual liberty, freedom of choice, and democracy, as well as on reforms based on Islam.

But the party also does not speak with one voice on pivotal issues. More than two decades after Islah's birth, the original strands remain distinct factions, which have often sparked serious internal debates over the party's role, its relationship with the government, and the scope of women's rights. The result is often ambiguous, confusing, or even conflicting policy statements.

THE BEGINNING

The roots of Islamist politics in modern Yemen date back to the 1960s with the birth of a local chapter of the Muslim Brotherhood. A second Islamist social movement emerged in the 1970s, when the country was still divided into rival halves. Muslim scholars in North Yemen, a secular autocracy with strong ties to the West, were concerned about threats from South Yemen, a Marxist and atheist state backed by the Soviet Union. The clerics, led by Sheikh Abdul Majid al Zindani, established a schooling system in the north to counter anti-Islamic movements and secular messages from the south.

Dubbed "scientific institutes," these schools resembled the *madrassas* that educated the young on the basis of religious texts in Pakistan and Afghanistan. The institutes provided room, board, and badly needed education for Yemeni youth, the majority of whom were illiterate. In turn, however, the institutes indoctrinated students in Salafist teachings inspired by Wahhabism, the strict ideology imported from neighboring Saudi Arabia. The schools grew to parallel Yemen's state education system, with summer camps and other activities to engage youth. Much as in Pakistan, many of the students educated in Zindani's institutes eventually went to Afghanistan in the 1980s to fight the Soviet occupation.

The Islah Party was founded after the May 1990 merger of North Yemen and South Yemen. President Saleh, who had only an elementary school education, fostered the party for his own political purposes. After working his way to power through the military, Saleh had been president of North Yemen from 1978 until 1990 and then assumed leadership of the unified Yemen as part of the deal to merge the two countries. Unification made Yemen a more powerful country, but it also widened the field of political players and opponents.

Saleh wanted a new Islamist movement to help his own party, the General People's Congress, check the potential of new political rivals. He especially hoped that Islah's greater theological and social legitimacy would counter the former ruling party of South Yemen, the Yemeni Socialist Party.

To launch Islah, Saleh enlisted Zindani and Sheikh Abdullah al Ahmar, chief of the northern Hashid Tribal Confederation—home of Saleh's clan and Yemen's largest tribal grouping. For Zindani, who brought along the Salafi network, the new party provided validation and a mainstream voice.

For Ahmar, Islah provided an institutional perch from which he could exert formal power to complement the respected but unofficial role accorded a tribal elder. Ahmar brought along other tribal and business associates to widen the party base.

The Muslim Brotherhood, which lacked any other political vehicle, became the third and largest strand to join Islah. Islah provided a comfortable home for the Brotherhood, even though the Muslim Brothers differed significantly from both Zindani and Ahmar. The Brothers were not Zindani acolytes, nor did they share his ultraconservative Wahhabi leanings. And the Brothers did not have steadfast tribal allegiances to Ahmar.

So from the outset, Islah was a diverse coalition of teachers, preachers, businessmen, and tribesmen with distinct and sometimes conflicting goals. Yet together these disparate strands of society partnered with the technocratic General People's Congress to rule Yemen from 1990 to 1997. In its first run for office in 1993, Islah won 62 of the 301 seats in parliament, and in 1997, it won 57 seats. After both elections, Ahmar was selected as speaker of parliament.

IN OPPOSITION

During its first seven years, Islah was dominated by its tribal and Salafi factions. But in 1996, during a party conference, the Muslim Brotherhood faction won control of the general secretariat. Four men aligned with the Brotherhood rose to the top: Mohammed Abdullah Yadoumi, Islah's secretary-general; Mohammed al Saadi and Abdulwahab al Anisi, his assistants; and Mohammed al Qahtan, who headed the Executive Council. The Brotherhood-oriented leaders quietly built the backbone of the party, happy to benefit from Ahmar's patronage but not acquiescing to the tribal scions.

The rise of the Brothers began the party's drift away from cooperation with the ruling General People's Congress. In 1997, Islah formally joined the opposition.

Ever the tribal chief, however, Ahmar kept his ceremonial post as speaker of parliament and his personal ties to Yemen's president. A local analyst described Islah as "developing the body of an opposition party with its head in the governing party," as Ahmar cooperated with Saleh while the rank-and-file membership increasingly looked like a Muslim Brotherhood political party.

The growing split inside Islah was evident during Yemen's first direct election for president in 1999. The original party founders—tribal leader Ahmar and Zindani, the Salafist—still supported Saleh, while key Brotherhood members rejected the traditionally cozy relationship. The Brothers calculated, however, that Saleh's election was a forgone conclusion. They opted instead to wait for a battle they might win—and began talking with other opposition parties.

The showdown played out in 2001 local elections as Islah competed openly against the ruling party, forgoing the usual negotiations over a guaranteed share of seats. In a seemingly odd pairing of Islamists and Marxists, the Brotherhood wing of Islah also launched quiet negotiations with the Yemeni Socialist Party.

The talks reflected the Islamist party's sense of realpolitik. Whatever its commitment to promoting Muslim values, Islah was willing to negotiate quite practically with parties antithetical to its own political doctrine. As a predominantly northern party, Islah also demonstrated willingness to work with a group from the south in the name of sheer political power.

Islah's initiative came at a political crossroads for the socialist movement, which was clearly in decline. The Yemeni Socialist Party and smaller leftist parties had boycotted the 1997 elections; by 2000, they faced political oblivion. President Saleh accused them of backing violent secession. He embarked on a campaign to deprive the socialist party of funding and confiscated many buildings it had controlled while ruling South Yemen.

Yet the Yemeni Socialist Party still had a powerful moral claim to be the voice of the south. It was also the most significant secular, leftist political faction in the country of 24 million people. The president's heavy-handed repression resonated with Islah leaders, who empathized with an underdog.

The avowedly secular socialists and the Islamists found common ground in demanding more freedom of speech and association and in arguing for better elections. In 2003, they began a unique political venture. With three other smaller players, they formed the Joint Meeting Parties on the premise that together they could defeat the ruling party. In 2006, the coalition fielded a joint candidate—a socialist—for president. Faisal bin Shamlan won 25 percent of the vote, a respectable outcome against the long-established and better-financed ruling party.

Islah also became increasingly pragmatic on issues, pushing back against ultraconservative measures. Its legislative priorities usually involved secular topics—electoral laws, economic policies or budget issues, parliamentary oversight, and constitutional questions about the distribution of local and regional power. It accepted the separation of mosque and state, rejecting an Islamic state or theocratic rule by religious sheikhs even as it promoted religious values based on Islamic law in politics.

But the Islamist party proposed few new laws on religious issues. Fewer than half of the questions formally addressed to the government by its members of parliament dealt with Islamic practices or traditions, such as banning alcohol. Islah's tangible achievements were still largely linked to in the social services where the party had started—religious education, welfare, and health care.

THE UNRAVELING

The death of Ahmar, "the sheikh of sheikhs," in December 2007 started Yemen's long descent into political gridlock. For almost a generation, he had been the political glue that had held together Islah's divided factions and propped up President Saleh. Ahmar's power always shaded the Islamist movement with a tribal character.

As paramount tribal leader, Ahmar had special standing, with more natural authority than a modern president. He was also chairman of Islah and speaker of parliament. All three titles effectively made him the second most powerful politician in Yemen. Only Saleh rivaled Ahmar's political authority. Indeed, because the state's actions often reflected tribal preferences, Saleh had to seek the sheikh's concurrence on any major endeavor. Saleh also did not dare directly confront Islah while the grand sheikh was alive. The president needed Ahmar's continued support when other Islah factions opposed him.

Ahmar, who reflected the contradictions at the heart of Islah, could also mediate among the party's religious and tribal factions. He often held together the delicate political truce through his status, authority, and force of personality. Despite their growing numbers, the Salafis were held at bay by Ahmar's reputation—and his private tribal army. And Islah's technocrats, who were aligned with the Brotherhood, were more interested in a disciplined modern party vying for power than in the medieval tribal machinations. But they too often deferred to Ahmar.

After Ahmar's death, Islah and other opposition groups in the Joint Meeting Parties grew bolder. In 2009, they formulated a "national salvation" plan to thwart the president and his ruling party. Islah then launched grassroots meetings countrywide to sell it. The party also called for a delay in the 2009 parliamentary elections. Its goal was to force the government to rewrite election laws and force Saleh to abide by term limits agreed to in 2006, which would have seen his rule end by 2012.

Saleh agreed to political reforms but asked that the parliamentary election be delayed from 2009 until 2011. Islah agreed, although it refused any further cooperation in an attempt to freeze Yemeni political life and weaken the president. Saleh countered with a campaign to vilify Yemen's political opposition parties as radicals.

Islah's political challenge coincided with two formidable security confrontations. The president also faced a rebellion in the north by the Shiite Houthi clan and an autonomy movement in former South Yemen that became known as the *Hirak*. Saleh began describing the Houthis as "Iranians," members of the Hirak as "secessionists," and Islah as "al Qaeda." He tried to portray himself as a comparative moderate and the stable alternative.

THE UPRISING

In January 2011, powerful shock waves from the uprisings in Tunisia, Egypt, and Libya reverberated into Yemen. Students organized mass demonstrations in University Square, which was soon dubbed "Change Square." The flashpoints were originally economic hardships, social injustice, and a constitutional amendment that could have extended Saleh's presidency. The central demand soon grew to include Saleh's ouster after more than three decades in power.

As with Islamist movements elsewhere, Islah leaders were slow to recognize the protests and reluctant to participate in Yemen's version of the Arab awakening. And when they did get involved, the party preferred to offer Saleh a negotiated exit rather than support the kind of coup that had toppled the leaders of Tunisia, Egypt, and Libya.

As pressure from the streets intensified, Islah Secretary-General Yadoumi began negotiating with the president and his allies to avoid violence. Saleh stalled. His government increasingly deployed force against the demonstrators. On March 18, at least fifty protesters were killed, a turning point that changed the character of protests and participants. A senior general responded by defecting to the opposition with his entire brigade. The addition of troops to the opposition encouraged a wider swath of the population—including many Islah adherents who had previously stayed home—to join the crowd.

As the crisis deepened and the death toll rose in cities across Yemen, Islah helped form a "committee of three" with members from the Yemeni Socialist Party and the ruling General People's Congress. For months, they sought to facilitate Saleh's departure and avoid Yemen's disintegration into a failed state. The six-nation Gulf Cooperation Council brokered the final terms. On November 23, 2011, Saleh signed a deal to end his thirty-four-year rule and hand over power to his vice president. His departure opened the way for all Yemen's opposition parties to expand their political sights.

KEY POSITIONS

Democracy

In Islah's official documents, religion is the backdrop, not the core, of a philosophy that often resembles classical liberalism more than theocracy. Its manifesto identifies seven basic principles: Islam as a belief and a life-governing law; justice; liberty; equality; *shura* (consultation) and democracy; a republican system; and republican unity.

Liberty, as described by Islah, is a "natural characteristic of man," who is "able to choose whatever desired of opinions and activities." *Democracy* means "participation in government and the people's right to decide on their affairs and choose their rulers, monitoring them and making them accountable and ensuring their adherence in the decisions they make." *Shura* is "to take the opinion of the people directly or through their representatives, so that no individual or one party monopolizes the state to the exclusion of others."

On democracy, Islah sometimes sounds more like Thomas Paine than Thomas Hobbes. Islamic law and Sharia, while invoked throughout the manifesto, are quickly qualified by references to democracy. "Peaceful rotation of authority is the essence of *shura* and democracy and the best process for overcoming conflict over authority—on all levels," intone the writers. Another plank says, "Sound political nurturing of members of society to grow accepting the results of elections and peaceful transfer of power."

Women's Rights

In its party constitution, Islah calls for measures to "rectify the inferior image of women" and to reform the "traditional" role of women, making them partners in all societal roles. In practice, however, its progressive-sounding policies have not been internalized by the grassroots. Many, if not most, male Islah members support a traditional housebound role for women.

"Good values and morals" in the family are described as a cornerstone of social cohesion, according to the party commands. Women should give priority to "their families by better upbringing of their children." Women are expected to "shoulder other family responsibilities, such as increasing the family income when needed."

Islah members have also voted differently on legislation. In 2009, the government proposed raising the minimum age of marriage for women from fifteen years to seventeen years, part of the effort to reform family law. Some Islah members voted for the amendment, while others claimed it contradicted Sharia.

Yet Islah has an exceptionally strong women's committee that takes a leading role in organizing its election activities, even though it is a conservative religious party. Women's leadership within the party is also strong. Tawakol Karman, the 2011 Nobel Peace Prize winner, is an elected member of Islah's Shura Council. Other prominent women leaders include Dr. Amat Al Salam Raja, who won more votes than Zindani when she ran for Islah's Shura Council.

During elections, small bands of Islah women, recognizable by armbands worn on the sleeves of their *abayas*, are often out canvassing voters, delivering leaflets, and convincing reluctant voters to go to the polls on election day. According to postelection surveys, Islah's efforts to court women have paid off.

Israel

Israel and Zionism get only passing references in Islah literature. In the preamble to Islah's manifesto, "Zionist endeavors" are described as one of the causes of "civilizational conflict," but Israel and the Palestinians are never specifically mentioned.

A shorter Islah election document in 2003 mentions "supporting the Palestinian's jihad and legitimate struggle against the Zionist occupation," but Islah has never shown any inclination to join causes or struggles outside

Yemen's border except in symbolic fashion. Islah has never pursued special links to Hamas or any other organization with a terrorist designation.

THE FUTURE

In 2012, Islah again joined the governing coalition in Yemen, pledging to stay until the transitional period ends in 2014. The party has strengthened its political position. At the same time, power in Yemen is more of a curse than a blessing.

Many Yemenis are skeptical of Islah's long-term intentions because of the party's ambivalence about the youth-led street protests and its strong tribal dynamic. The party sometimes appears to be a modernizing force but at other times looks more like a conservative tribal coalition determined to protect the status quo. It is also still unclear whether Islah understands youth discontent and can harness it in policies and actions after the end of President Saleh's rule. Islah's willingness to work effectively with leaders of the General People's Congress, particularly technocrats in ministry positions, is a strength, but it also breeds distrust among the youth.

As part of the coalition, Islah faces a chronically weak economy further damaged by months of conflict. Water and resource shortages threaten large population centers. And a series of intractable tribal conflicts have inhibited foreign investment, damaged critical infrastructure, and stunted social development. The post-Saleh government has to counter three security challenges: an increasingly antagonistic and assertive al Qaeda branch in southern Yemen, the southern Hirak secession movement, and the northern rebellion by the Shiite Houthi clan.

Yet Islah is part of a wide-ranging coalition that includes southern moderates, tribal leaders, and technocrats. To stabilize Yemen, the transition government's top domestic priority will be trying to convince the Houthis and the more radical members of the Hirak to join efforts to rebuild Yemen. The transition government will also, however, need investments or aid from the international community to prevent the Arab world's poorest country from becoming a failed state.

Leslie Campbell is senior associate at the National Democratic Institute and regional director for the Middle East and North Africa. Since 2009, Campbell has made twelve trips to Yemen to discuss issues of political reform and dialogue among political factions as an alternative to conflict.

CHAPTER 14

Turkey: The New Model?

Ömar Taşpinar

In the twenty-first century, Turkey is arguably the most dynamic experiment with political Islam among the fifty-seven nations of the Muslim world. It also offers seminal lessons for the Arab world, despite the tense history (especially during the Ottoman Empire) and many differences.

Turkey's ruling Justice and Development Party (AKP) went through five incarnations before it found a balance that voters would embrace but the military would also accept, albeit reluctantly. Its evolution reflects how democratic traditions and institutions can both interact with and moderate political Islam, at least in one geostrategic country. In Turkey, a tradition of free and fair elections and capitalism has encouraged Islamic parties to play by the rules. Turkey's radical secularism, enforced by the military, has also tamed the strident religious dogma that once landed Islamic politicians in trouble—and even in prison.

The AKP is a political party with clear Islamic roots. It pragmatically moved to the center-right over a decade, mainly to escape the fate of its defunct predecessors. The party's success, however, has had little to do with ideological factors. Turkish voters have been primarily concerned with bread-and-butter issues. In June 2011, they once again voted for political stability and rewarded Prime Minister Recep Tayyip Erdoğan for the country's growing prosperity and better social services, particularly in health care and housing.

The victory for the AKP was historic. It was only the second time since the beginning of Turkey's multiparty democracy in 1946 that a political party had won three consecutive elections. And it was the first time that a party actually increased its percentage of the vote at each succeeding election. The AKP received 34.28 percent of the vote in 2002. It won 46.58 percent in 2007. And it scored 49.90 percent in 2011.

It was a striking reversal. All previous Islamist parties in Turkey had been shut down by either military intervention or rulings by the constitutional court: The National Order Party, founded in 1970, was banned by the Constitutional Court in 1971. The National Salvation Party, founded in 1972, was outlawed after the 1980 military coup. The Welfare Party, founded in 1983, was banned by the Constitutional Court in 1998. The Virtue Party, founded in 1997, was banned in 2001.

Turkey is notable because its Islamist parties have reemerged, more moderate and pragmatic, after each closure. "Autocratic regimes in the Muslim world often ban religious parties, which then go underground and turn violent. Turkey's Islamists have taken a different path. Despite being repeatedly outlawed and ejected from power, pious politicians have shunned violence, embraced democracy, and moved into the mainstream," The Economist noted in 2008. "No Islamic party has been as moderate and pro-Western as the AKP, which catapulted into government in 2002 promising to lead Turkey into the European Union."

Erdoğan, who founded the party, actually rejects defining the AKP in religious terms. "We are not an Islamic party, and we also refuse labels such as Muslim-democrat," he said in 2005. The AKP leader instead calls the party's agenda "conservative democracy."

The AKP's journey from political Islam to conservative democracy is not just the result of political expediency or respect for the red lines of Turkish secularism. The evolution of Turkey's capitalism under the leadership of Turgut Özal in the 1980s created an entrepreneurial Muslim bourgeoisie in the conservative heartland of Anatolia. The new Muslim bourgeoisie had a greater stake in politics—and became more engaged.

These "Islamic Calvinists" have been more concerned about maximizing profits, creating access to international currency markets, and ensuring political stability than about introducing Islamic law or creating a theocracy. Turkey now has thousands of such small and medium-sized export-oriented businesses, often referred to as "Anatolian tigers." Most support the AKP. Beginning in the 1990s, the party's assumption of political power gradually moderated the radical elements within Turkish political Islam.

The AKP leadership clearly views the party as a model for other Muslim countries. On June 12, 2011, Erdoğan told thousands who had gathered to celebrate the AKP's landslide victory, "Sarajevo won today as much as Istanbul. Beirut won as much as Izmir. Damascus won as much as Ankara. Ramallah, Nablus, Jenin, the West Bank, [and] Jerusalem won as much as Diyarbakir."

THE BEGINNING

The rise of Islamic politics in Turkey was in large part a reaction to the traumatic birth of a modern state after the Ottoman Empire collapsed following World War I. Since the 1920s, Turkey's official ideology has been Kemalism, which grew out of the ultrasecular views of Mustafa Kemal Atatürk, the founder of the Turkish Republic. The Kemalists pursued a top-down project of radical modernization. In an ambitious drive to import European civilization, the republic disposed of the governing caliphate, the Arabic alphabet, Islamic education, and the Sufi brotherhoods that were an important part of both religion and culture.

Kemalist Turkey adopted Western legal codes from Germany, Italy, and Switzerland, together with the Latin alphabet and the Western calendar,

Western holidays, and Western dress. The country's official history and language were reworked. A new education system glorified pre-Islamic Turkic civilizations at the expense of the country's more recent Ottoman past, and many Arabic and Persian words were purged to create an "authentically" Turkish vocabulary. Even the Arabic *azan*, the call to prayer, was no longer allowed in its original form and had to be chanted in modern Turkish, to the dismay of pious Muslims.

Yet despite massive reforms, secular Kemalism barely infiltrated Turkish society at large. The rural and pious masses of Anatolia remained largely unaffected by the cultural reengineering in Ankara, in contrast to the military, the bureaucracy, and the urban bourgeoisie, who embraced or adapted to Kemalism's superficial Westernization. The cultural gap between the Kemalist center and the Anatolian periphery soon became insurmountable. A Kemalist slogan in the 1920s acknowledged that the Turkish government ruled "For the people, despite the people."

Religious conservatives and ethnic Kurds actively opposed the Kemalist mission to create a Westernized, secular, and homogenous Turkish nation-state. Between 1923 and 1938, the new Kemalist government unleashed its military to suppress a series of Kurdish and Islamist rebellions.

Turkish politics entered a new era after 1946. When the Cold War divided up the world, Turkey's decision to turn toward the West and join the North Atlantic Treaty Organization (NATO) fostered a transition to multiparty democracy—and a realignment of political forces between left and right. Kurdish discontent found its place in the socialist left, while political Islam was part of the anticommunist right. Behind the scenes, the military remained a powerful force. It intervened in 1960, 1971, and 1980 to restore a sense of Kemalist order against both leftist and conservative parties.

But in 1991, after the Cold War ended and communism collapsed, Turkey's identity problems rapidly resurfaced. The right and left were no longer able to absorb the passions of Kurdish and Islamic dissent. Turkey was polarized along two axes: Turkish versus Kurdish identity on the one hand, and Islamic versus secular identity on the other. The result was the "lost decade" of the 1990s—a decade of war with Kurdish separatists, polarization over the role of religious values, economic turmoil, and unstable coalition governments.

ISLAMIST VICTORIES

In 1994, the Welfare Party—the third incarnation of the pro-Islamist Party—shocked the Kemalist establishment by winning local elections nationwide and capturing control of Turkey's two largest cities, Istanbul and Ankara. The party was headed by Necmettin Erbakan, who had close connections with Egypt's Muslim Brotherhood. After seven decades, Turkey's secular tide was ebbing. A year later, the Welfare Party won the largest bloc in parliamentary elections, putting an Islamist-led coalition in charge of the entire country.

The Welfare Party's victory was short lived. Alarmed that the new government would adopt an overtly Islamic agenda, the military stepped in. Turkey's generals feared that the government would suppress secular opposition, allow Islamic dress in universities, and abandon Turkey's Western alliances. In fact, however, the Welfare Party actually adhered to most mainstream Turkish political practices. It did try to plant sympathizers in ministries it controlled, but so had many previous governments. Still, the secular press warned of an imminent Islamist revolution.

On February 28, 1997, the military—with wide backing from civil society and the secular media—forced Erbakan and his party out of power. The bloodless coup had major unintended consequences. It spurred serious soul-searching among Turkey's Islamists, eventually sparking a generational and ideological rift within the movement.

The Welfare Party's pragmatic young leaders—notably Recep Tayyip Erdoğan (not to be confused with Erbakan) and Abdullah Gül—recognized the red lines of Turkish secularism. (Erdoğan, then mayor of Istanbul, learned the hard way. In 1999, he spent four months in jail for reciting a poem with Islamic undertones.) After participating in democratic politics for more than three decades, Turkey's Islamists had already tempered their views to win a wider following at elections. By the late 1990s, political Islam was ready to fully integrate into mainstream politics.

In 2001, Erdoğan created the Justice and Development Party, the fifth and final incarnation of the pro-Islamist party, from the ashes of the dissolved Welfare Party and the Virtue Party. He crafted the term conservative democracy—rather than an Islamic reference—to explain his political agenda. He understood that political liberalization would consolidate the AKP's power base.

To achieve two crucial objectives, Erdoğan put democratic reforms at the top of his agenda, seeking to comply with European Union (EU) membership guidelines. The move earned him the support of Turkey's business community, liberal intellectuals, and pragmatic middle class. It also won him political legitimacy in the eyes of the military. After all, European recognition had long been the ultimate prize in Atatürk's vision of a Westernized Turkey. And by giving priority to social services, the AKP also appealed to the impoverished underclass. Erdoğan's strategy paid off. In November 2002, the party won the largest bloc of seats in the parliamentary elections.

REFORMS

Between 2002 and 2006, the AKP government passed a series of reforms to harmonize Turkey's judicial system, civil-military relations, and human rights practices with European norms. Through its formidable grassroots network and with governmental institutions now in its hands, the party made health care and housing credits more accessible, distributed food, increased grants for students, improved the infrastructure of poorer urban districts, and made minority rights for Kurds and non-Muslims a priority.

Reforms were not confined to politics. The party also managed to get the Turkish economy back on track after the economic crisis of 2001 by following International Monetary Fund guidelines.

Between 2002 and 2011, the Turkish economy grew by an average rate of 7.5 percent annually. Lower inflation and interest rates led to a major increase in domestic consumption. And the Turkish economy began to attract unprecedented foreign direct investment, thanks to a disciplined privatization program. The average per capita income rose from $2,800 U.S. in 2001 to around $10,000 U.S. in 2011, exceeding annual income in some of the new EU members.

Yet even as the AKP adopted a more liberal order, Kemalist segments of Turkish society grew increasingly suspicious that it had a hidden agenda. They feared that the AKP was exploiting the EU membership process to diminish the military's political role and, eventually, the Kemalist legacy. They balked, for instance, at AKP measures to increase the ratio of civilians to military officers on the National Security Council, elect a civilian to head the National Security Council, remove military representatives from the boards of the Council of Higher Education and the Radio and Television High Council, and grant broadcasting and cultural rights to Kurds.

On foreign policy, Prime Minister Erdoğan's willingness to compromise on the question of Cyprus also polarized Turkish politics. The AKP backed a United Nations plan to reunify the island; the military adamantly opposed the plan. The deadlock was an important obstacle to EU membership—and the pro-Islamist party actually appeared more willing to compromise than either the secularists or the military. A subsequent investigation revealed that a military coup over the Cyprus question was barely averted in 2004 because of divisions among the Turkish generals.

POLARIZATION

Turkey's internal divisions deepened between 2006 and 2008. The AKP had long wanted to lift the ban on Islamic dress—or wearing of headscarves—in universities and end discrimination against graduates of Islamic high schools (such as special criteria for their university entry exams). The AKP had strong popular support for both steps. More than 50 percent of Turkish women covered their heads.

Party leaders preferred to promote reform by building a national consensus rather than by challenging the secularist establishment head-on. But secularists remained wary. They pointed to Erdoğan's brief attempt to criminalize adultery in 2004, his appointment of religious conservatives to bureaucratic positions, and AKP attempts to discourage the sale of alcohol.

Tensions between the AKP and the military climaxed after Erdoğan announced he would nominate Foreign Minister Abdullah Gül for the presidency. The presidency is a prestigious though ceremonial post—but also the last bastion of secularism in the eyes of the military and the opposition.

On April 27, 2007, the generals staged the country's first "e-coup." They posted a warning on the military's website that "if necessary, the Turkish Armed Forces will not hesitate to make their position and stance abundantly clear as the absolute defenders of secularism." Given Turkey's history of military interventions, the note was a thinly veiled threat that a more conventional coup might be in the offing.

In a sign of the AKP's growing self-confidence, Erdoğan did not back off. He instead decided to defy the generals by calling early elections. The AKP won a landslide victory in mid-2007 with almost 47 percent of the votes—compared with 34 percent in 2002 when it came to power. The election was a public rebuke to the generals.

The AKP crowned its victory when parliament elected Gül to the presidency. But the military shadow still loomed over Turkey. The top brass stayed away from the inauguration. And in 2008, Turkey's chief prosecutor tried to have the AKP closed on grounds that it pursued an Islamist agenda to subvert the secular republic. The party survived this "constitutional coup" attempt by a whisker. The court voted against closure by just one vote.

CONSOLIDATION

Between 2008 and 2011, the AKP consolidated its gains. Despite the political turbulence, Turkey weathered the global financial crisis of 2008 with remarkable success. The economy continued double-digit growth rates in 2009, after a brief recession. By 2012, Turkey's unemployment rate and budget deficit were at record lows.

In June 2011, the AKP won its third consecutive electoral victory with nearly 50 percent of the vote. The country's global stature also reached new heights. As uprisings shook the Middle East, reformers in Egypt, Jordan, Libya, Morocco, Syria, and Tunisia often cited Turkey and the AKP as models.

The AKP also consolidated its supremacy over the military—a first since the creation of the modern state. On July 29, 2011, the military's chief of staff resigned after a disagreement with Erdoğan about staff promotions. The same day, the heads of the army, navy, and air force requested early retirement. By early 2012, half of all Turkish admirals and one out of ten active-duty generals were in jail for plotting against the government. It was a paradigm shift for a country that had experienced three military coups and constant military meddling for almost a century.

KEY POSITIONS

Democracy

The AKP heralds democracy; its more seasoned politicians have participated in free elections for two decades. But Turkey remains polarized, with its opposition parties ever more concerned about creeping authoritarianism and Islamism. Opponents call the government a civilian dictatorship and deplore its use of the judicial system to neuter the military, the opposition media, and rival political parties.

Opposition fears are reflected in the court case against Ergenekon, a shadowy organization with possible ties to the military. The judiciary launched the case in 2007, shortly after AKP's second electoral victory, claiming that Ergenekon had planned a coup. The prosecutor accused hundreds of military officials, journalists, and political activists of involvement. Leaked documents claimed the Ergenekon network was tied to several bombings and assassinations, which were intended to create chaos and justify a military coup. AKP critics contended that the Erdoğan government used the case to silence its secular opponents. The AKP responded that it did not control the judiciary—which had even tried to ban the party as recently as 2008.

Minorities

The status of Turkey's Kurdish population has been the AKP's Achilles' heel. Kurdish aspirations have been thwarted largely by legal and political obstacles that are the remnants of the 1982 constitution written under military rule. Despite the AKP's rhetorical commitment to deal with Kurdish expectations, Erdoğan has not spent the political capital needed to expand the limited political space for Turkey's ethnic groups. He now seems to have resorted to the classic Turkish mantra that there can be no democratization when the country is facing terrorism. As a result, violence has only grown in the Kurdish southeast.

Women's Rights

The AKP has done nothing formal to alter women's rights. To the contrary, by pushing for EU membership and harmonizing Turkish laws with European standards, the AKP has eliminated some of the legal obstacles that discriminate against women in the labor market and civil code. But the AKP is also clearly a conservative and patriarchal political party. Erdoğan's understandings of family values and gender equality are not progressive.

Until recently, the restraints of Turkey's strong secular constitution impeded observant Muslim women more than secular females. Women who wear *hejab*, or head covering, were banned from official events and public university classes, for example. Erdoğan sent his two daughters, who cover their hair, to American universities abroad because they could not attend Turkish colleges. In 2011, the AKP changed the legislation dealing with dress codes in public universities and legalized *hejab*. The restrictive dress code for civil servants, however, remains in place.

The West

AKP leaders claim that membership in the European Union is their strategic priority. Yet the AKP has demonstrated growing self-confidence by expanding Turkey's reach and diplomatic relations beyond the West. The EU's reluctance to embrace Turkey formally and the European economic crisis have also led the AKP to look to the Middle East, Africa, Russia, and Central Asia as areas where Turkey can exert soft power—what Turkish Foreign Minister Ahmet Davutoğlu called Turkey's "strategic depth." Analysts dubbed the activist Turkish foreign policy "neo-Ottomanism."

Yet the AKP had almost no problems in Turkey's relations with the United States. "Americans used to ask: Who lost Turkey? Now they are busy asking questions about the success of [the] Turkish model," a senior AKP official quipped. The AKP even decided to host NATO radar installations needed for the new U.S. missile-defense system against Iran.

Israel

For decades, Turkey had the closest relations of any Muslim state to Israel. Under the AKP, Erdoğan even mediated briefly between Israel and Syria during 2007 and 2008. The AKP foreign policy generally sought "zero-problem with neighbors." But as the AKP deepened Turkey's ties to Iran and the Hamas government in Gaza—including AKP efforts to facilitate humanitarian aid to Gaza—tensions deepened with Israel. Erdoğan also once called Syrian President Bashar al Assad his "brother," although after the Syrian uprising began in 2011, Turkey called for Assad to step down. Erdoğan also opened Turkey for Syria's opposition summits, defecting soldiers, and refugees.

By 2012, Turkey instead seemed to have "zero neighbors without problems," a senior diplomat said, because of growing problems with neighboring Syria, Iran, and Israel.

THE FUTURE

Under the AKP, Turkey is still not a liberal democracy, despite the pattern of multiparty elections. Compared to the lost decade of the 1990s, however, it has become a more multifaceted democracy, with elections, public opinion, opposition parties, parliament, the media, and civil society all exerting more power. For the first time in the republic's history, Turkey's performance is also totally in civilian hands. The military, once empowered to check civilian politics, is no longer strong enough either to step in or to threaten to take action. And the party with Islamic roots has undertaken more reforms required for EU entry than any of Turkey's secular parties.

The AKP government feigned modesty about its standing in the Islamic world. "We are not presenting ourselves as a model," Erdoğan told an audience of Turkish journalists in 2011. "Maybe we are a source of inspiration or a successful example in some areas." Yet Turkey's experience with Islamist politics—no longer simply an experiment—was widely cited both inside and outside the Muslim world.

By 2012, however, the AKP had also exposed serious democratic shortcomings. It increasingly cracked down on its critics, especially those in the media. After a decade in power, Erdoğan had also failed to follow through on promises of a new constitution and reforms that would address pivotal issues facing the country—the Kurdish question, human rights, and freedom of expression. Because of mounting Kurdish terrorism and Erdoğan's populist instincts, the more power Erdoğan won at the polls, the less interested he appeared in taking those steps.

Ömer Taşpinar is professor at the National War College and senior nonresident fellow at the Brookings Institution. He is the coauthor of Winning Turkey: How America, Europe, and Turkey Can Revive a Fading Partnership *(2008). His website is http://www.brookings.edu/experts/taspinaro.aspx.*

CHAPTER 15

Islamist Groups: Parties and Factions

Annika Folkeson

Islamist groups in the Arab world are diverse in their political agendas, goals, and activities and thus defy simple categorization. But several trends and common denominators have emerged in the early twenty-first century.

In 2012, the Arab world has more than fifty Islamist or pro-Islamist parties. Almost half have been formed over the past decade. The groups are both new and old. The largest dates back to 1928; at least ten were formed only in 2011. Some parties have wide experience and deep social networks; others are starting from scratch.

The positions of several parties have evolved over time or because of political realities. But very few parties could be described as moderate. Most are conservative to ultraconservative in their social agendas. The vast majority of Islamist parties want Sharia law to be an essential part of the new order, but they diverge widely on how strictly or how quickly to implement it.

Many parties claim to support "democracy" or "pluralism," but their positions often fall seriously short of real democratic values. For many of them, democracy means participation in multiparty elections and coexistence with other religious minorities, but the parties often fall short of those goals on specific issues such as minority rights, gender issues, and the extent of civil liberties.

Many parties have emerged from rigid ideologies or strict interpretations of Islamic law, but frequently there are gross inconsistencies between tough party platforms and the toned-down comments of senior officials in interviews. Members often have disparate opinions. Party websites and programs describe lofty democratic goals—such as on women's rights—that are not reflected in practice. Many parties limit their advocacy on women's rights to the reform of personal status law, which affects family issues such as the right to divorce, child custody, and inheritance.

In the sectarian landscape of the Middle East, no mass parties appeal broadly to both Sunnis and Shiites. Yet even within the same sect, many movements are actually rivals, such as the Muslim Brotherhood and Nour Party among Sunnis in Egypt or the Dawa Party and Islamic Supreme Council among Shiites in Iraq.

On economic policy, many parties support private enterprise and capitalism but almost inevitably want a strong emphasis on "social justice" in terms of a more equitable distribution of national resources. Even when they were outlawed, many of these movements gained popular support through networks of social services, which they favor expanding once they are in power.

Like many of their secular counterparts, the Islamist groups take strong positions in support of a Palestinian state. Many support Hamas and the use of violence or "resistance" against Israel. But some groups, such as Egypt's Islamist groups, have said that they will honor international treaties, an implicit commitment not to abrogate the Camp David peace treaty with Israel. On ties with the United States, even those who talk to American diplomats want to diminish U.S. influence in their countries.

Of the more than fifty Islamist parties in fourteen Arab countries, the largest number emerged directly or indirectly out of the Muslim Brotherhood. The Brotherhood has a presence or offshoot in most Arab countries, although the shapes, leadership types, agendas, and names vary.

In Egypt, Jordan, and Syria, the movement has existed as an opposition force for many decades. In a few of the Gulf countries, where political parties or religious groups operating outside the state's religious authorities are not permitted, the Brotherhood exists more as a strand of influence than as an organized political group. In Bahrain, the Brotherhood is openly affiliated with the regime; in Kuwait, the Brotherhood is a main political group.

The most dynamic new political players are Salafi groups, which have increased across the region in the twenty-first century, particularly after the Arab uprisings. Salafi groups account for the second largest number of Islamist groups in the Arab world. They have traditionally renounced a role in politics, even tolerating autocratic leaders as long as they were Muslims. But Salafis, too, differ broadly even within countries, where Salafi groups are often the sum total of several gatherings around local sheikhs rather than a single national movement.

This list includes more than fifty Islamist or pro-Islamist movements, ranging from centrist groups and Salafi ideologues to elected parties that still rely on both the ballot and the bullet. The list does not include apolitical movements, purely militant groups, or smaller parties.

ALGERIA

Movement of Society for Peace

History: Founded in 1988 by Mahfoud Nahnah, the Movement of Society for Peace (Harakat al Moujtama as Silm, or MSP) is now led by Aboujerra Soltani. The MSP is a branch of Egypt's Muslim Brotherhood and has participated in several governments.

Positions: The 2007 platform proposed that a grand mufti serve as the chief legal authority, but the party does not call for Sharia law or an Islamic state. The party supports women's rights to education and work, but it does not advocate changing the conservative Family Code. It supports Islamic banking, social welfare, and state control of certain sectors. But the party encourages private investments in the oil sector and the promotion of small and medium-sized enterprises. The MSP supports the Palestinian cause and calls for the return of all Palestinian territory. It pulled out of the governing coalition in January 2012, saying this is "the year of competition—not alliances."

Website: http://www.hmsalgeria.net/

Justice and Development Front

History: Founded in 2011 by Abdallah Djaballah (also a founder of the Islah and Ennahda parties, now largely inactive), the Justice and Development Front (FJD) was legally recognized in 2012 but did not immediately publish a political platform.

Positions: The FJD is socially conservative, and it attracts Salafi supporters.

Website: http://eladala.net/ar/

National Front for Change

History: The National Front for Change was founded in 2009 by Abdelmajid Menasra, previously a leader in the Movement of Society for Peace. In early 2012, it was not yet legally authorized.

Positions: The Front called for amnesty for former members of the Islamic Salvation Front and criticized Algeria's undemocratic system.

Movement for National Reform

History: The Movement for National Reform (al Islah) is the successor to Ennahda, also founded by Abdallah Djaballah. After Djaballah's departure in 2006, the party lost significant support.

Islamic Salvation Front

History: Founded in 1989 by Abbasi Madani and Sheikh Ali Belhadj, the Islamic Salvation Front (FIS) won the first round of parliamentary elections in 1991. In 1992, a military coup aborted the election and outlawed the FIS, which sparked a decade-long insurgency. The FIS renounced violence in 1999. In 2011, parliament sustained the ban on the FIS. The organization is currently led from exile by Madani.

Positions: The FIS calls for an Islamic state but accepts multiparty elections. It emerged as a Salafi movement with strict interpretation of Sharia law and gender segregation.

Website: http://fisdz.com/

Others

Ennahda, the predecessor to the FJD and the National Front, was formed in the 1980s but is now largely inactive.

The Movement for Liberty and Social Justice was founded in 2007, led by former FIS leaders, most of them in exile. They have been seeking without success to convince the military that they have forsworn violence and truly embraced multiparty democracy.

BAHRAIN

Islamic National Accord Association

History: A Shiite party founded in 2001, the Islamic National Accord Association (Wefaq) is Bahrain's largest party, led by Sheikh Ali Salman. In 2009, Abdul Jalil Maqdad and Abdul Wahab Hussein split from Wefaq and founded the Wafa Islamic Party, which has yet to be legalized.

Positions: Wefaq is socially conservative and emphasizes Islamic values, but it supports multiparty elections. In 2011, Wefaq's eighteen members of parliament resigned to protest regime violence against protestors.

Website: http://www.alwefaq.org/

Authenticity

History: Authenticity (Asalah) was founded in 2002 and is led by Ghanim al Buaneen.

Positions: Asalah is the main Salafi political party in Bahrain. It promotes a hardline interpretation of Islam that rejects Western political and cultural influence. The party officially supports women's rights, but Buaneen has said that the party opposes women's political participation. Asalah views Shiites as heretics, but it sometimes cooperates with the Shiite party Wefaq on morality issues. Asalah opposed U.S. military action in Iraq and supports the Palestinian cause.

Website: http://www.alasalah-bh.org/main/

Platform

History: Founded in 2001 with close ties to the regime, the Platform (Menbar) is led by Salah Abdulrahman. It is the political wing of the Islah Society, which is associated with the Muslim Brotherhood, formed in 1941.

Positions: Menbar seeks to strengthen Islamic values and social equality. It allows women's political participation, but in the 2006 election, Menbar chose not to field any female candidates because its conservative ally, Asalah, opposed it. Menbar backed a women's campaign to reform the personal status law.

Website: http://www.almenber.org/

Islamic Action Party

History: The Islamic Action Party (Shirazis) was founded in 2002 and led by Sheikh Mohammad Ali al Mahfudh, who is currently in jail. One of the main Shiite Islamist parties, the Shirazis originated as the militant Islamic Front for the Liberation of Bahrain. The Shirazis boycotted the 2010 elections because of arrests of its members. The party supported the 2011 demonstrations.

Positions: The group focuses on political and human rights and rejects sectarianism. It calls for an Islamic state based on Sharia law.

Website: http://amal-islami.net/

Haq Movement

History: Another splinter group from Wefaq, Haq was founded in 2005 by Hasan Mushaima but is not legalized. The regime accused Haq of using violent tactics. Its leaders were jailed in 2011.

Positions: Haq boycotted the 2006 and 2010 elections and rejects engagement with the regime. It supports the antiregime protests.

EGYPT

Muslim Brotherhood and Freedom and Justice Party

History: Founded in 1928 by Hassan al Banna, the Muslim Brotherhood is the world's largest Islamist movement with more than eighty branches. First organized as a social movement, the Brotherhood then went through a radical phase from the late 1940s to the 1960s, when Sayyid Qutb was a leading ideologue. Officially banned in the 1950s during the Nasser era, it renounced violence in 1969 and has fielded independent candidates for parliament since the 1980s.

In 2011, it launched the Freedom and Justice Party, led by Mohammed Morsy. In the 2011–12 elections for parliament, the party won a plurality with 43.4 percent of the vote as part of the Democratic Alliance coalition.

Positions: The party supports Sharia law as the source of legislation but advocates a civil state, not a theocracy. It would grant the Constitutional Court the right to oversee legislation to ensure compatibility with Islamic principles. On worship and personal status, non-Muslims would live under their own laws or traditions. Brotherhood members have voiced diverse opinions on Israel, minorities, and women's rights. On its website, the party states that "peace treaties with Egypt can only be valid if passed by a referendum of the people," but in 2012 the party said it would honor Egypt's international treaties. In 2007, it said neither Coptic Christians nor women should be eligible to become president. But in 2012, the Brotherhood said that while it would not nominate either to be president, it would honor the will of the Egyptian majority.

Website: http://www.hurryh.com/

Nour

History: Founded in 2011 and led by Emad Abdel Ghaffour, Nour is the main Salafi party and the second largest party. It was the first of three members of the Islamist Bloc alliance, which included the Building and Development Party and Asala. Together, they won 27.8 percent of the vote in the 2011–12 elections.

Positions: A socially conservative party, Nour emphasizes social justice and calls for a civil state, but it seeks the gradual implementation of Sharia law. It officially supports democracy, although senior officials have said that democracy is a form of apostasy. Nour says that religious, personal status, and family issues for Coptic Christians should be handled by Coptic religious traditions. Nour officially supports women's rights, but its leaders advocate gender segregation in education and public spaces. It fielded women as candidates largely because of electoral law but used flowers or party symbols instead of their faces on election material. It supports a state-led economy but also the protection of private property. In July 2011, Nour said it would hold a referendum on the peace agreement with Israel, but in December 2011, Nour said it would uphold the treaty but possibly modify parts of it.

Website: http://www.alnourparty.org/

Building and Development Party

History: The Building and Development Party (Bana wa Tanmiya) was founded in 2011 by Tareq al Zumr and Safwat Abdul Ghani as the political party of the Islamic Group (al Gamaa al Islamiyya), a former militant group linked to Anwar Sadat's 1981 assassination and attacks on security forces, tourists, and Coptic Christians. It renounced violence in 2002. The second of three parties in the Islamist Bloc alliance, it won 2.6 percent of the vote in the 2011–12 elections.

Positions: A socially conservative party, Bana supports multiparty elections in a political system based on Sharia. On women's rights, the party says it wants to "solve the problem of rising marrying age and the increasing number of divorces." It seeks a "socially just" economy but encourages private investment. Bana rejects Westernization, and it wants to reduce foreign influence in the economy. The party says it will uphold international agreements as long as they do not oppose Islamic principles or popular will. It supports an independent Palestinian state. In January 2012, a senior party member said that he would welcome al Qaeda leader Ayman Zawahiri back to Egypt.

Websites: http://tinyurl.com/44kqruc, http://benaaparty.com/default.aspx, and http://www.egyptianislamicgroup.com/en/

Wasat Party

History: Founded in 1996 by Aboul Ela Madi, Wasat is a breakaway faction from the Muslim Brotherhood. It was not legalized until after Mubarak's ouster. It won 1.8 percent of the vote in the 2011–12 parliamentary elections.

Positions: A progressive Islamist party, its ideology stems from the centrist (Wasatiya) school of Islamic thought. Wasat calls itself a "civil" party with an Islamic frame of reference that supports multiparty elections. It advocates a free market and encourages private investment. Wasat supports gender equality and inclusion of all religious minorities. It fielded sixty-nine women and two Coptic Christians on its electoral lists. It supports the Palestinian cause and the right of resistance to the Israeli occupation, but it does not seek to revoke or amend the Camp David accords.

Website: http://www.alwasatparty.com/

Authenticity

History: Authenticity (Asala) was founded in 2011 by Adel Abdul Maksoud Afify, Ihab Sheeha, and Mahmoud Sultan. Salafi Asala, the third party in the Islamist Bloc, won 0.6 percent of the vote in the 2011–12 elections.

Positions: Asala seeks to spread Islamic values and restore Egypt's leadership globally. It believes in the strict application of Sharia law, gender segregation, modest Islamic dress, and prohibition of alcohol. Asala's program states that political and economic international agreements should be revised. The party rejects recognition of Israel but reportedly does not seek to nullify the peace treaty with Israel.

Virtue

History: Virtue (Fadila) was founded in 2011 by Mahmoud Fathi and Mohammed Maksoud Afify. Afify then left the party and joined Asala. Fadila was initially part of the Democratic Alliance but withdrew before the 2011–12 elections because of party infighting and did not field any candidates.

Positions: The Salafi party calls for an Islamic state. It seeks press freedom but protection of moral values. Fadila does not oppose a relationship based on dialogue with the United States and Israel. The party supports an independent Palestinian state but does not wish to nullify the peace agreement with Israel.

Website: http://www.alfadyla.com/

Egyptian Current Party

History: The Egyptian Current Party (Tayyar al Masry) was founded in 2011 by Mohamed al Kassas, Islam Lotfy, and Ahmed Abdul Gawad, prominent members of the Muslim Brotherhood's youth wing. Tayyar was part of the Revolution Continues electoral alliance, which won 1.6 percent of the vote in the 2011–12 elections.

Positions: A more moderate Islamist party, Tayyar supports a civil state and the protection of individual civil liberties. It embraces Islamic values but does not seek the enforcement of Islamic law.

Website: http://www.tayarmasry.com/

Reform and Renaissance Party

History: Founded in 2011 by a small group of independent Islamists and led by Hesham Mostafa Abdel Aziz, the Reform and Renaissance Party did not win any seats in the 2011–12 elections.

Positions: The Reform and Renaissance Party calls itself a "civil" party that seeks to revitalize religious values. The party supports free market principles and privatization. It seeks an end to the Israeli-Palestinian conflict and ambiguously talks about maintaining relations with neighboring countries on the basis of dialogue. It favors cooperation with Europe and the United States.

Website: http://www.eslah-nahda.org/eslah/

IRAQ

Islamic Dawa Party

History: The Islamic Dawa Party was founded in 1957 by Shiite clerics and led by Prime Minister Nouri al Maliki. Shiite Dawa initially promoted Islamic values and political awareness through education programs and demonstrations. After the 1968 coup, Dawa was repressed and became increasingly militant. It renounced violence in the 1990s.

Positions: Dawa's platform does not call for an Islamist state, and the party has increasingly moved toward more secular language and positions. It emphasizes both religious values and democratic principles, although critics note Dawa's increasingly authoritarian tendencies and repression of the opposition under Maliki. The party supports women's participation in politics, but only one out of forty-two cabinet posts is now held by a woman. Dawa favors a free market economy.

Website: http://www.islamicdawaparty.com/

Sadr Movement

History: This movement merged as a Shiite political force in 2003 and was led by the cleric Moqtada al Sadr. His powerful Mahdi Army militia, which targeted U.S. forces and rival Iraqi groups, was officially disbanded in 2007. A mass movement, it provides social services and youth education programs and has strong support among poorer Shiites. In the 2010 parliamentary elections, Sadrists allied with the National Iraqi Alliance, which won 21.5 percent of the vote.

Positions: The Sadr Movement calls for an Islamic state and Sharia law. Initially more of a social than a religious movement, the Sadr Movement champions rights of the Shiites, the largest population group but long repressed under earlier Sunni rulers. It has been accused of attacking Internet cafes, DVD shops, and unveiled women. But the party supports women's participation in politics and successfully fielded female candidates that exceeded the set quotas. Sadr is close to Iran, where he studied religion during part of the U.S. intervention. The Sadr Movement is fiercely anti-American and anti-Israeli.

Website: http://www.alsadronline.net/en/

Islamic Supreme Council of Iraq

History: The Islamic Supreme Council of Iraq (ISCI) was founded in 1982 in Iran by Mohammed Baqr al Hakim. It is now led by his nephew, the cleric Ammar al Hakim. The Shiite political party is the largest member of the Iraqi National Alliance, which won 21.5 percent of parliamentary seats in 2010. Its militant wing, the Badr Organization, broke away and established its own party but allied with ISCI in the 2005 and 2010 elections.

Positions: ISCI does not call for an Islamic state but wants Sharia law as the main source of legislation. ISCI supports multiparty elections. In 2007, ISCI indicated an ideological shift away from Iran and the rule of the jurisprudent (*Wilayat al Faqih*) by dropping *revolution* from its name and expressing loyalty to Iraqi Grand Ayatollah Ali al Sistani instead of Iran's

Supreme Leader Ayatollah Ali Khamenei. The party supports women's political participation and has fielded female candidates in elections, but it opposes the quota system. It wants to restrict alcohol consumption and Westernization. Despite its close relationship with Iran, ISCI cooperates with the United States.

Websites: http://www.isci-iraq.com/ and http://www.almejlis.org/

Iraqi Islamic Party

History: Founded in 1960 and modeled on the Muslim Brotherhood, the Iraqi Islamic Party (IIP) is now led by Osama Tawfiq al Tikriti and Mohsen Abdul Hamid. Once the largest Sunni Islamist party, it lost support after Iraqi Vice President Tariq al Hashimi left the IIP in 2009 to create the Renewal List, a secular party that joined the Iraqiyya electoral alliance.

Positions: The IIP has become more nationalist than Islamist; it does not call for an Islamic state but promotes Islamic values. The party briefly suspended contacts with U.S. officials in 2008, accusing U.S. troops of targeting its members.

Website: http://www.iraqiparty.com

Others

The Shiite political party Virtue (Fadila), part of the Iraqi National Alliance in 2010 elections, is led by Ayatollah Muhammad Yaqubi. Fadila has fifteen seats in parliament and controls the provincial council of Basra.

The Association of Muslim Scholars is not a political party but previously had significant political influence. The group has lost support in recent years.

There are several smaller Kurdish and Turkmen political parties, some of which are Islamist. The Islamic Union of Kurdistan, with ties to the Muslim Brotherhood, competed independently in the 2010 elections. Another influential Islamist group is the Kurdistan Islamic Group.

JORDAN

Muslim Brotherhood and Islamic Action Front

History: Formed in 1945, the Muslim Brotherhood fielded its first candidates in 1989 as independents. The Brotherhood has worked within the political system but its relations with the regime have been tense in recent years. Its political party, the Islamic Action Front (IAF), was founded in 1992 and is currently led by Hamzeh Mansour.

Positions: Initially, the Brotherhood called for Sharia law, but it did not seek an Islamic state or oppose the monarchy. The IAF supports multiparty elections. As recently as 2007, the IAF called for implementing Sharia law and supported segregated classrooms, mandatory veiling for women, and a ban on alcohol. Women have held seats on the IAF consultative council, but the IAF does not support gender equality through legal reform. The IAF is a peaceful opposition group that may protest government policies, such as the peace treaty with Israel, but fully accepts Hashemite rule. The IAF supports creation of a Palestinian state, but the Brotherhood also supported the regime's repression of Palestinian groups in 1970. The IAF is a critic of U.S. policies in the region.

Website: http://www.jabha.net/

Wasat Party

History: Founded in 2003 and led by Haitham Amayreh, the Wasat Party is a small, centrist party of independent Islamists who left the Islamic Action Front because of the Muslim Brotherhood's dominance. It cooperates with several secular parties.

Positions: Wasat is more moderate than the Islamic Action Front. It views Sharia's role in legislation as flexible and supports democratic principles. Female members of the party have participated in elections and hold leadership positions in the party. The party is open to engagement with the United States and Europe.

Website: http://www.wasatparty.org/

Liberation Party

History: Founded in Jerusalem in 1952, the Liberation Party (Hizb al Tahrir) is an international Sunni Islamist movement. The organization does not usually participate in elections and is banned in many Arab countries. In 1952 and 1992, the organization applied for legal status as a political party but was rejected both times.

Positions: The Liberation Party is a socially conservative organization that seeks to establish a caliphate. The organization does not support democracy, which it views as a Western concept, or gender equality.

Website: http://www.hizbuttahrir.org/

KUWAIT

Islamic Constitutional Movement

History: Founded in 1991 by Jassem Mohalhel and now led by Nasir al Sani, the Islamic Constitutional Movement (Hadas) is the political wing of Kuwait's Muslim Brotherhood, which was formed in 1952. Political parties are illegal in Kuwait and are usually referred to as *societies*.

Positions: Hadas calls for a gradual implementation of Sharia law through a consultative process.

Website: http://www.icmkw.org/

Islamic Salafi Alliance

History: The Islamic Salafi Alliance was founded in 1981 and is led by Abdul Rahman al Mutawa.

Positions: It seeks to implement Sharia law and establish an Islamic state. The group opposes women's participation in politics.

Umma Party

History: The Umma Party (Hizb al Umma) is a Salafi party founded in 2005 by Hakem al Matairi. The government refused to legalize the party, and its founders were accused of plotting to overthrow the government.

Positions: Matairi said that the party was established to promote pluralism, transfer power through peaceful means, and implement Sharia law. But the party has criticized the democratic provisions of Kuwait's constitution.

LEBANON

Hezbollah

History: Founded in 1982 under Iranian tutelage, Hezbollah is a Shiite Islamist movement led by Sheikh Hassan Nasrallah. Hezbollah is a religious, political, and military movement that provides extensive social services; it is on the U.S. list of terrorist groups. Hezbollah's military wing is estimated to be the second largest military force in Lebanon, after the army. It carried out several suicide bombings and kidnappings in the 1980s and 1990s and fought an open war with Israel in 2006. Hezbollah has participated in elections since 1992 and joined the government in 2005.

Positions: Hezbollah favors an Islamic state but has also said that it recognizes the complications in Lebanon's multisectarian setting. The group is allied with the largest Christian party. Women hold midlevel positions within the party, but it has not fielded any female candidates for parliament. Hezbollah's militia engaged in a thirty-four-day war with Israel in 2006. In its 2009 manifesto, Hezbollah "categorically" rejected reaching any compromise with Israel or recognizing its legitimacy "even if everyone else recognizes 'Israel.'" It views the United States as its enemy but has interacted with European countries.

Website: http://www.moqawama.org/

The Islamic Society

History: Founded in 1964 and led by Ibrahim al Masri, the Islamic Society (Jamaa al Islamiyyah) was inspired by the Muslim Brotherhood. It is the second most important political player among Sunnis and provides extensive social services. It has run candidates in elections since 1992, although it is not a political party.

Positions: Jamaa seeks to establish an Islamic state, which it acknowledges would be difficult in multisectarian Lebanon. The group supported Hezbollah's war against Israel in 2006.

Website: http://www.al-jamaa.org/index.php

Society of Islamic Charitable Projects

History: The Society of Islamic Charitable Projects was founded in 1980 by Sheikh Abdallah al Harari as a Sunni Islamist umbrella organization ambivalent about political participation. It had Syrian backing during Syrian rule in Lebanon but is now allied with the pro-Western Mustaqbal movement.

Islamic Action Front

History: The Islamic Action Front (Jabhat al Amal al Islami) was founded in 2006 by Fathi Yakan, also a cofounder of al Jamaa al Islamiyya, who died in 2009. It is a Sunni Islamist movement. Yakan split from Jamaa in 2006 because of its alliance with the Mustaqbal movement, which it believes serves Western interests.

Others

The Salafist movement, founded in 1946 by Sheikh Salem al Shahhal, has grown to include some fifty organizations operating charities and schools. The Salafis historically had not participated in Lebanese politics. But after the 2005 killing of former Prime Minister Rafik Hariri and Syria's withdrawal from Lebanon, the Salafis began mobilizing their followers to vote.

LIBYA

Muslim Brotherhood and Libyan Islamic Group

History: Founded in 1949, the Muslim Brotherhood is the largest and best-organized Islamist group in Libya. At its first national conference in Libya, the movement elected Bashir Kabti as leader in late 2011.

Positions: The Brotherhood announced that it would form a party that aims to establish a "civil state with Islamic references" and has encouraged women to participate in politics.

Libyan Islamic Movement for Change

History: The Libyan Islamic Movement for Change was founded in 2011. Led by Abdelhakim Belhaj, the Sunni group was established from the remnants of the outlawed militant Libyan Islamic Fighting Group (LIFG), which renounced violence and was disbanded in 2010. Belhadj was the military commander of the LIFG, which trained with al Qaeda in Afghanistan but did not come under its umbrella.

Positions: The group advocates Sharia law as the principal source of legislation.

Others

Prominent religious authorities such as the cleric Ali Sallabi and Sheikh al Sadiq al Gharyani have large followings, but they have yet to establish political parties. Sallabi spent several years in prison under Moammar Qaddafi's rule. Gharyani was the former head of the Supreme Council for Fatwas under Qaddafi but is seen as politically independent.

MOROCCO

Justice and Development Party

History: Founded in 1997 when the Sunni party first ran in elections, the Justice and Development Party (PJD) is now led by Abdelilah Benkirane. The largely co-opted opposition party won 27 percent of the vote in the 2011 parliamentary election and now heads the government. But its political influence is limited because the king still holds religious and political supremacy.

Positions: Socially conservative, the PJD accepts the monarchy and does not seek to establish an Islamic state. Its positions on democracy, women's rights, and religious freedom are ambiguous and often contradicted by members' statements. Overall, the party has gradually adopted a secular discourse. The PJD voted for reforms favoring women in the personal status code, which was not exclusively based on Sharia law, as a concession to the monarchy and public sentiment.

Website: http://www.pjd.ma/

Justice and Charity

History: Founded in 1987 by Sheikh Abdessalam Yassin, a Sufi leader, Justice and Charity (Adl wa Ihssan) has been outlawed since 1990. The movement has a strong grassroots presence in universities and Islamic charities.

Positions: The socially conservative group does not recognize the legitimacy of the monarchy and stays aloof from politics. It seeks radical change of the political system and advocates a democratic state with Sharia law as the main source of legislation. Women are allowed to participate in politics and Yassin's daughter Nadia Yassin heads the women's branch.

Website: http://www.aljamaa.net

PALESTINIAN AUTHORITY

Hamas

History: Founded by Sheikh Ahmed Yassin in 1987 during the first Palestinian uprising, Hamas (Harakat al Muqawama al Islamiya) is now led by Khaled Mashaal. Hamas grew out of the Muslim Brotherhood and is the most influential Palestinian Islamist group. It is a social movement, a militia, and a political party. It is on the U.S. list of terrorist groups for carrying out attacks and suicide bombings in Israel. After rejecting participation in elections for decades, Hamas ran in local elections in 2004 and won the 2006 parliamentary elections.

Positions: Hamas defines itself as a centrist (*wasatiyya*) movement, which implies a moderate approach and a gradual application of Islamic principles. It has increasingly democratized internal procedures, holding leadership elections. It supports women's participation in politics; six of its female candidates won seats in the 2006 election and women sit in the party's ruling council. But many Hamas members favor gender segregation. The group rejected participation in the Oslo peace process in the 1990s and opted instead for violent resistance. It does not accept Israel but says it will accept a Palestinian state that is based on the 1967 borders. Hamas has often mentioned a possible long-term truce. The party has had informal contact with several European countries, and its leadership has said it is willing to talk with the United States.

Website: http://www.hamasinfo.net

SYRIA

Muslim Brotherhood

History: Founded in 1946 by Mustafa al Sibai, the Muslim Brotherhood is now led by Mohamed Riad al Shaqfe. The Brotherhood has participated in elections since 1947 but was banned in 1963. Membership in the Brotherhood has been punishable by death since 1980, when violent struggles took place between the Islamist group and the regime. It forms the largest bloc in the opposition Syrian National Council.

Positions: The Brotherhood seeks the gradual implementation of Sharia law but a civilian pluralist state. A 2004 document says that power should be reached through the ballot box, but its position on the role of religious scholars in politics is ambiguous. Syria's current Sharia-based legal framework would continue to be the reference for women's rights in family matters. The Brotherhood supports the rights of religious minorities and does not seek to change the current personal status law for Christians. The movement advocates a market-oriented economy. It does not recognize Israel, but it is open to further engagement with the United States and Europe despite its criticism of U.S. policies in the region. The movement renounced violence in 2001.

Website: http://www.ikhwansyria.com/ar/

Movement for Justice and Development

History: Founded in London in 2006 by Anas al Abda and Osama al Munajjid, the Movement for Justice and Development (Harakat al Adala wal Bina, or MJD) is active among the exiled opposition and holds 5 out of 310 seats on the opposition Syrian National Council.

Positions: Inspired by the ruling Justice and Development Party in Turkey, the conservative party highlights Syria's Islamic identity but does not seek implementation of Sharia law. The people's will is the only source of legislation. The MJD has engaged extensively with Western governments.

Others

The Syrian National Movement (Tayyar al Watani al Suri) includes both liberals and Salafis. It was founded in late 2011 in Cairo. The group holds twelve seats on the opposition Syrian National Council.

The Democratic Independent Islamic Trend (Tayyar al Islami al Mustaqill al Dimuqrati) is a network of moderate Islamic activists, most of whom were based in Syria until March 2011 but have since left Syria.

TUNISIA

Ennahda

History: Founded in 1981 by Rachid al Ghannouchi, Ennahda was outlawed and repressed under President Zine al Abidine Ben Ali. In the 1989 election,

Ennahda fielded independent candidates, who won more seats than did small secular parties. In 2012, it was the largest party, winning over 41 percent of the vote for the constitutional assembly in 2011.

Positions: The party does not call for Sharia law or an Islamic state. Ennahda supports multiparty elections and Ghannouchi has written extensively on Islam's compatibility with democracy. He called for Jewish Tunisians to return and emphasized support for minorities. Ennahda has said it will not change the current Personal Status Code for women, and it was the first party to support an equal number of women and men on electoral lists. Ennahda has criticized U.S. policies in previous decades—particularly policies regarding Palestine—but it seeks a cooperative relationship with the West. It does not seek active involvement in the Palestinian issue. In 2011, the party opposed an effort to outlaw normalization of relations with Israel.

Website: http://www.nahdha.info/arabe/

Others

The Salafi group Followers of Sharia (Ansar al Sharia) was founded in April 2011 by Sheikh Abu Ayyad al Tunisi. Since the 2011 uprising, several Salafi student and social groups have emerged. The Salafis seek an Islamic state and Sharia law. They reject political parties and democratic elections, support gender segregation and public prayer on university campuses, and favor modest Islamic dress.

TURKEY

Justice and Development Party

History: Founded in 2001 by Recep Tayyip Erdoğan, the Justice and Development Party (AKP) is currently the ruling party after winning elections in 2002, 2007, and 2011. The AKP is often described as the world's most successful Islamist party and is a source of inspiration for movements across the Middle East. It is the fifth incarnation of earlier Islamist parties that were closed by the Constitutional Court because of their religious platforms. When the Islamist Virtue Party was banned, the reformists formed AKP and the hardliners established the Felicity Party.

Positions: The AKP calls itself a secular party with a socially conservative platform and Muslim values. The party has a substantive record of supporting democracy. More than any secular party, it has undertaken the democratic reforms necessary to comply with entry into the European Union and the liberal economic policies that have boosted growth. But the party has also begun to crack down on opposition media. Critics contend the AKP wants to "Islamize" Turkey, citing its attempts to criminalize adultery. The party has been pragmatic in dealing with Israel and has strong bilateral trade ties despite growing friction in recent years.

Website: http://www.akparti.org.tr/

Felicity Party

History: Founded in 2001 by Recai Kutan and Necmettin Erbakan, the Felicity Party (Saadet Partisi) has roots in previous Islamist parties that were outlawed because of their religious platforms. The party did not pass the 10 percent threshold to win seats in parliament in the 2011 elections.

Positions: Felicity is more conservative than the AKP in terms of women's rights, the role of religion in the public sphere, and economic policy. The party led protests against the Israeli intervention in Gaza in late 2008 and has been harsher than the AKP in criticism of Israel.

Website: http://www.saadet.org.tr/

YEMEN

Yemeni Congregation for Reform

History: The Yemeni Congregation for Reform (Islah) was founded in 1990 by Sheikh Hussein al Ahmar and Sheikh Abdul Majid al Zindani, a Salafi cleric labeled a terrorist by the United States in 2004. The party is the political arm of the Muslim Brotherhood, which emerged in the 1960s. Islah has been in and out of government since 1990, sometimes allying with leftist opposition parties.

Positions: Islah seeks social reform that is based on Islam. In 2007, the Brotherhood's more pragmatic members won a power struggle against ultraconservative Salafis. Women are allowed to participate in politics and several prominent women, such as the 2011 Nobel Peace Prize winner Tawakol Karman, hold party leadership positions. But grassroots elements of the party would prefer women to remain in more traditional roles. Islah supports the Palestinian cause, though it is not a primary concern of the party.

Website: http://www.al-islah.net/

Annika Folkeson works for the Center for Conflict Analysis and Prevention at the U.S. Institute of Peace. She previously worked for the International Foundation for Electoral Systems in the Palestinian territories. She has also worked in Syria and Lebanon.

Contributors

Christopher Alexander is the John and Ruth McGee director of the Dean Rusk International Studies Program at Davidson College. In addition to several articles on politics in North Africa, he is the author of *Tunisia: Stability and Reform in the Modern Maghreb* (2010).

Khalil al Anani is a scholar of Middle East politics at the School of Government and International Affairs at Durham University in Britain. His books include *Elections and Transition in the Middle East in the Post-revolutionary Era* (forthcoming), *Religion and Politics in Egypt After Mubarak* (2011), *Hamas: From Opposition to Power* (2009), and *The Muslim Brotherhood in Egypt: Gerontocracy Fighting against Time* (2008).

Nicholas Blanford is the Beirut correspondent for *The Times of London* and *The Christian Science Monitor*. He is the author of *Killing Mr. Lebanon: The Assassination of Rafik Hariri and Its Impact on the Middle East* (2006) and *Warriors of God: Inside Hezbollah's Thirty-Year Struggle against Israel* (2011).

Nathan J. Brown is professor of political science and international affairs at George Washington University. He is also a nonresident senior associate of the Carnegie Endowment for International Peace. His most recent book is *When Victory Is Not an Option: Islamist Movements in Arab Politics* (2012). His website is http://home.gwu.edu/~nbrown.

Leslie Campbell is senior associate at the National Democratic Institute and regional director for the Middle East and North Africa. Since 2009, Campbell has made twelve trips to Yemen to discuss issues of political reform and dialogue among political factions as an alternative to conflict.

Annika Folkeson works for the Center for Conflict Analysis and Prevention at the U.S. Institute of Peace. She previously worked for the International Foundation for Electoral Systems in the Palestinian territories. She has also worked in Syria and Lebanon.

Abdeslam Maghraoui is associate professor of political science at Duke University and member of the Duke Islamic Studies Center. He is author of *Liberalism without Democracy* (2006) and a series of papers on the challenge of democratization in the Maghreb. He studies comparative politics of the Middle East and North Africa with a focus on the interplay between culture and politics.

Manal Omar is the director of the North Africa, Iraq, and Iran programs for the United States Institute of Peace. She was a member of the Libya Stabilization Team under the National Transitional Council formed during the revolution. She was previously a regional program manager for Oxfam GB and led humanitarian responses for Yemen, Lebanon, the Palestinian Territories, and Iraq. Omar is the author of *Barefoot in Baghdad* (2010).

David B. Ottaway lived in Algiers from 1962 to 1966 while working for UPI and *The New York Times*. A former *Washington Post* Middle East correspondent, he coauthored with his wife, Marina, *Algeria: The Politics of a Socialist Revolution*. He visited Algeria again in 2009 and 2010 for a book about his life and times as a foreign correspondent. He is a public policy scholar at the Woodrow Wilson International Center for Scholars.

Thomas Pierret is a lecturer in contemporary Islam at the University of Edinburgh. He is the author of *Baas et Islam en Syrie* (2011); the English version, titled *Religion and State in Syria*, will be published by Cambridge University Press. His blog in French is http://blogs.mediapart.fr/blog/Thomas%20Pierret.

Olivier Roy, a professor at the European University Institute in Florence, is the author of *Globalized Islam* (2004) and *Holy Ignorance* (2010). He heads the ReligioWest Research project at http://www.eui.eu/Projects/Religio West/About/.

Jillian Schwedler is associate professor of political science at the University of Massachusetts, Amherst. She is the author of *Faith in Moderation: Islamist Parties in Jordan and Yemen* (2006) and coeditor of *Policing and Prisons in the Middle East* (2010). Her website is http://polsci.umass.edu/profiles/schwedler_jillian.

Samer Shehata, an assistant professor at Georgetown University, is a former fellow at the Woodrow Wilson International Center for Scholars, the National Endowment for the Humanities–American Research Center in Egypt, and the Carnegie Foundation. He is the author of *Shop Floor Culture and Politics in Egypt* (2009) and the editor of the forthcoming *Islamist Politics in the Middle East: Movements and Change* (2012).

Ömer Taşpinar is professor at the National War College and senior nonresident fellow at the Brookings Institution. He is the coauthor of *Winning Tur-*

key: How America, Europe, and Turkey Can Revive a Fading Partnership (2008). His website is http://www.brookings.edu/experts/taspinaro.aspx.

Robin Wright is a joint fellow at the Woodrow Wilson International Center for Scholars and the U.S. Institute of Peace. A former correspondent for *The Washington Post*, her most recent book is *Rock the Casbah: Rage and Rebellion Across the Islamic World* (2011). Her blog is http://robinwrightblog.blogspot.com and her book website is http://www.robinwright.net.

Index